Canute's Tower

St. Beuno's

1848 - 1989

Canute's Tower
St. Beuno's
1848 - 1989

Paul Edwards

Gracewing.

Fowler Wright Books
Southern Avenue
Leominster HR6 0QF

Gracewing Books are distributed

In Canada by	*In Australia by*
Novalis	Charles Paine Pty
PO Box 990	8 Ferris Street
Outremont H2V 457	North Parramatta
Canada	NSW 2151 Australia

First published by Fowler Wright Books 1990

ISBN 0 85244 151 7

Typesetting by Print Origination (NW) Ltd, Formby, Merseyside L37 8EG
Printed and bound in Great Britain by Billings & Son, Worcester

Contents

Randal Lythgoe
Portrait at Mount St. Mary's, Spinkhill.

Map of St Beuno's College and the surrounding Area.

Gerard Manley Hopkins

Foreword

Umberto Eco once said that a title should not dragoon one's ideas, rather it should throw them into confusion. My title was not chosen to confuse, but it is meant to be enigmatic. Canute is for me an ambiguous figure. Was he so obtuse as to imagine that he could interdict the tide? Or did that astute and highly successful ruler deliberately set out to provide an unanswerable demonstration of his own impotence before the rhythmic onset of the sea?

Is the history of St. Beuno's a parable of wrong-headed resistance to the tide of change or is it an inspiring tale of men who read the flood and rode it to their chosen destination? Or is it perhaps both?

In telling this story I have had three separate audiences in mind. I have assembled a continuous narrative of St. Beuno's for my brethren of the British (formerly English) Province and taken some trouble to describe the old, institutional world of the larger scholasticate which the younger members of the Province have never known. The second at which I have aimed, consists of the many people who come here on retreat knowing something about St. Ignatius and the Exercises, very little about the English Province and nothing at all about St. Beuno's past, except that there is a connection with the poet Hopkins. Finally, I have looked beyond these groups to the many readers of that renowned poet who have only the vaguest notions about Jesuits and none at all about the English Province and St. Beuno's part in its history.

The 'onlie begetter' of this work is my Superior, Fr. David Brigstocke, who suggested that I tackle it, and has gently and persistently urged me on throughout a difficult year. The Director, Fr. William Broderick, freed me sufficiently from other work in the house to make it possible. My colleagues have borne with the moods engendered by my solitary days in the basement library, living, as I have so often said to them, the life of a pit pony.

The pleasantest part of the whole enterprise was to experience the extraordinary generosity of Peter L'Estrange S.J. of the Australian Province, who is preparing a doctorate on the Jesuits of the period, and made available to me the Aladdin's cave of his beautifully organised researches. Fr. Holt, the Province archivist, was his habitually courteous, knowledgeable self. A host of people have answered questions and supplied useful information. Miss Yvonne Davies, Librarian of Llanelwy (St. Asaph) and Rhuddlan has deployed the resources of the Clwyd libraries for me, and both read and corrected the typescript. Mrs. Menna Mair MacBain read the work chapter by chapter as it crawled from the typewriter to test its intelligibility for a non-Jesuit. Mrs. Sandra Hallett nee Wynne of the North Wales Arts Association exercised the same brief for the non-Papist. The one drawback about having completed this book will be that I shall need another reason to go on inviting these ladies to lunch or tea in the refectory, to which neither Fr. Lythgoe nor Fr. Hopkins would have dared to introduce them. And the shade of Canute will smile.

The Tower from the hillside

Trio on the tower

'Say something', I said to the judge, 'which I can quote in my book'. There was silence. The good and learned judge was at a disadvantage. After all, he had just scrambled up the steep ladder which leads to our tower, and squeezed his tall frame through a doorway forty inches high to emerge onto the duckboards, and be met with my crisp demand.

There was mischief in my request. Throughout a long and agreeable lunch he had discoursed amusingly and fluently on whatever subject was raised. Admittedly he had been somewhat vague when I wanted to know exactly at what period imprisonment became a routine legal penalty, but the ready flow of words quite concealed from the rest of the company how unsubstantial his answer really was. I had listened with appreciative relish to the mixture of anecdote, serious observation and elucidation of technicalities together with the vivid reconstruction of courtroom scenes. Though not quite contemporaries, he and I had attended the same inner city grammar school and were of the same immigrant stock, a connection which, I thought, gave me leave to test his eloquence to the limit.

I had found it. My fellow Liverpudlian looked me ruefully in the face and gracefully acknowledged defeat. 'What a way', he said, 'to reduce one to silence'. Immediately I reverted to the role of courteous guide, indicating the beauty of the countryside and the structure of the house in which it is my privilege to work.

St. Beuno's is built into the side of Moel Maenefa, Hopkins' 'pastoral forehead', one of the hills of the Clwyd range which descend like so many massive, roughly arranged stepping stones, from Moel Fammau nine miles away down to the Irish Sea at Prestatyn six miles to the north of us. From Prestatyn the long line of the sea sweeps westward to Llandudno twenty miles away with its Great and Little Ormes. These two unevenly matched promontories begin a chain, not just of hills, but of hills massed against hills, of mountains lying behind the hills, and mountains behind the mountains, until on a clear day Snowdon itself can be discerned thirty miles from us. The view to the south is much restricted by trees taller than the house itself—they were surely less tall in Hopkins' day—the last object we can see being the town of Denbigh, shrewdly sited on high ground and controlling the roads which lead over the high moors beyond it. Between Denbigh and the sea stretches our northern half of the Clwyd valley centered on the small town of St. Asaph (Welsh name: Llanelwy), which, because of its mediaeval cathedral, I should have termed a city, at the risk of completely misleading the reader as to its scale.

The beauty of it all, valley and hill, mountain and sea, has been celebrated in the poetry of G.M.H., almost half of which was composed at St. Beuno's. As he wrote in a letter to his mother: 'The valley looked more charming and touching than ever; in its way there can hardly be anything in the world to beat the vale of Clwyd.' To me our valley, broad, placid and rich looks English rather than Welsh, but the hills to the west belong to a more grudging terrain, to the harsher, less governable world of the Celt. Certainly the history of the region fits my ethnic interpretation of its geography. For centuries this was a no-man's land across which the Welsh fought the Saxons, resisted the Anglo-Norman magnates and were finally worn down by the Plantagenet kings. Behind St. Beuno's, across the face of Moel Maenefa, runs Offa's Dyke Path where the power of that formidable King of Mercia (757-96) reached its limit. At the mouth of the Clwyd in 921 King Edward, son of Alfred, reared a fort. Close by, at Rhuddlan, Earl Harold defeated Gruffydd ap Llewelyn. After Harold's own defeat and death (no need for a date here) the Norman Earls of Chester made Rhuddlan their base during the seesaw border warfare of the next two centuries. Here too, Edward I established his headquarters for the successful campaign of 1277 and received the submission of Llewelyn ap Gruffydd. Rhuddlan Castle, of which much still stands, was completed in 1282 and proved its worth a century later, when Owain Glyndwr, having burned the cathedral at St. Asaph and sacked the township of Rhuddlan, found himself powerless against its castle.

I let the judge gaze his fill on the landscape. Then I drew his attention to the tower itself. I told him how originally, before the north wing was added, the tower stood squat and square at the north west corner of the building, apparently bidding defiance to all who approached on those two sides. I drew his attention to the arrow slits which pierce the parapet at regular intervals of four feet, and to the kitchen archway far below to the right, which appears to be fitted with a portcullis. Actually this 'portcullis' is merely a curved piece of wooden trellis fixed into the archway, but it was certainly intended to suggest a portcullis. Why arrow slits and portcullis? Was someone amusing himself with fantasies of a Glyndwr redivivus raiding across the Clwyd once again? Hardly, for there is nothing else playful about our solid, solemn, markedly monastic, neo-gothic structure! Or is the use of a resurrected mediaeval style, admittedly very common for religious buildings in the nineteenth century, itself indicative of a fantasy, of an unwillingness to acknowledge the Renaissance, the Reformation, the Enlightenment and above all the Revolution? Are the arrow slits and portcullis the playful symptoms of a more serious evasion of reality?

Whatever their attitude to the present or past the men who built this house took it for granted that they were part of the future. That other men after them would see the world in the way they saw it, and want to do the same things in the same way. Their building was meant to last, and so it has for a hundred and forty years. Each January sees a new burst of effort on our part to adapt the interior to our present activities.

Yet in this building, and particularly on its tower, I am always brought face to face with the irresistibility of change. When I arrived at this house for the first time I was a youth of seventeen, and needed to shave only on alternate days, if then. I became a novice two years later, and was duly hatched out as a fledgling Jesuit with new taken vows. I arrived again at the age of thirty three, my academic feathers now full grown, but my general plumage still in need of the spiritual preening which we call the tertianship. After the tertianship we were judged fit to take our final flight away from the training aviaries of the Society. Now in my seventh (seven for completeness?) decade I roost here once more, my crest white, my pinions capable only of slow, short, arthritic flight. I have many memories and few expectations. I am grateful that I can still clamber to the tower and stare at the sea, to which I could once walk in an afternoon, and at the far hills amongst which I once covered twenty six miles in half a morning and a long afternoon. I now give myself to the less strenuous activity of watching 'the lovely behaviour of silk-sack clouds',

observing how 'the pattern is new in every moment'. I also come
by night, sometimes as late as midnight, stepping lightly on the
duckboards lest I disturb some retreatant in a room below. I am
there to reverence the stars, poetry and starlight being two of the
three created elements which move my 'deep magics'.

I became a stargazer during the war years. Being exempt from
military service, we eagerly demonstrated our patriotism by com-
plying meticulously with all government regulations. Sunday afternoons saw us walking through the country lanes carrying
our civilian gasmasks. The dark hours found us firewatching.
Throughout the night, pair relieving pair, two of us stood ready to
give the alarm, should the Luftwaffe shower St. Beuno's with
incendiaries. The obvious lookout point was the tower. From it I
watched 'the dappled-with-damson west'; I studied the slow, slow
coming of the dawn, and during the hours between saw the even
slower wheeling of the constellations, their brilliance enhanced by
the total blackout beneath.

'Non sum qualis eram'. It is more than the colour of my hair
and my restricted movement which separate me from the novice
of seventeen and the largely untried priest of thirty three. It is not
a matter of knowledge acquired, for so much of that has been
subsequently lost; nor of experience gained, so much of which has
since become irrelevant. It is one's perspective which has changed.
A change of perspective? Would it were that simple. It is, rather,
an accumulation of subtle shifts of perspective, some trifling,
others Copernican, each with its practical consequences for one's
ways of living and acting. Looking back I can clearly see that
the transformation of my theology of the priesthood (strictly
orthodox), the evolution of my liturgical outlook, and my gradual
conversion on the subject of the eucharistic ordination of women
(not considered orthodox) were truly 'Copernican' changes. The
fact that I find myself even more romantic in outlook at sixty
six than at thirty three, though personally gratifying, entails
little consequence for others beyond my startling the occasional
retreatant by reading poetry aloud, or surprising some woman
visitor by plucking her a shapely rose.

Stones however do not undergo a change of mental perspective;
they are reshaped only by chisel and drill, or by the majestic
powers of wind, sea or rain operating over centuries. Externally
therefore, this building remains virtually unaltered since the days

of Hopkins. But what of the typical 'inmate'? Have the inhabitants been as resistant as the stone? Earlier I suggested that the very structure and style of the building implied an unreal attitude to the past on the part of its creators combined with a fine confidence that the same formula of life would be followed by succeeding generations. Have those same attitudes been maintained however?

Here I must introduce, rather belatedly, the third person on the tower. She had been our hostess at lunch, but the tower found her largely silent. Perhaps this was because she knows the view well, being a regular and particularly welcome visitor. When I was a novice, and even when I was a 'tertian', a woman visitor was not admitted beyond the 'parlours', which were as close as possible to the front door. To bring her further into the house was a matter for excommunication. One of my contemporaries had the misfortune to fall from a room in the tower and the astounding luck to escape with mild concussion. As a precaution he was ordered to stay in bed with as little movement as possible. His anxious mother came to see him. Unfortunately the Rector, who alone could have given the lady permission to enter 'enclosure', was absent. The ignominious—some people would say 'jesuitical'—solution was to lift the young man into an invalid chair and wheel him through the corridors to one of the interview rooms.

Hence the presence on the tower of a lady, and one who was familiar with the entire building and on first name terms with everyone living in it, was for me like a banner flown aloft symbolising a St. Beuno's markedly different from that of my youth and early priesthood. Why the tower? Would not a woman in the dining room or one hanging up her clothes in the communal drying room be equally significant? I choose the tower, not merely out of a romantic preference for the lady on the battlements over the woman at the washing machine, but because for me associations and significance cluster around the tower like swarming bees about their migrant queen. There, confronting the same landscape as at seventeen and paying my respects to the same constellations, I am uniquely aware of 'the force that through the green fuse drives . . .' Aware also of the ebbless tide of physical, mental and temperamental change which has been at work in my own life . . .

More largely, the position of the tower dominating, as it once did, the northern approach and western flank, speaks to me of resistance, of resistance to the contemporary world, and of a will to maintain that resistance, assured that throughout the foreseeable future the defences would continue to be manned. No consciousness there of being 'soft sift in an hour glass', of being 'mined with a motion', of the need at times to run very fast in order to stay in the same place, of the need to alter one's language to say the same thing! Or do I read far too much into the whim of an architect and the acceptance by those who commissioned him of what was after all a contemporary taste?

I must now try, without prejudgement, to set forth in outline a hundred and forty years of the house's history, siting it as best I can in that Heraclitean flux of which everything under the sun and all human beings are a part. It may even be possible to peer tentatively into the future. In that notoriously fallible pursuit we may go less astray if we have a clear vision of past and present.

I

One man in a castle

First let me introduce a fellow romantic. The setting is the upper room of a castle in Spain in which he lies, a stricken hero slowly recovering from the wounds which have brought him close to death. No tower, I fear, because the defences of the castle were destroyed in 1457 and the rebuilding had to conform to a royal edict of 1460 that it be 'flat without towers or fortifications'.

It is 1521 and we are in the Basque country. The warrior is Inigo (later called Ignatius) de Loyola and it is with him, and at this point in his life, that the story of St. Beuno's really begins. The men for whom St. Beuno's was built, the men who taught, studied and worked there, were all, until very recently, Jesuits—members of the Society of Jesus which Inigo was to found.

When we meet him he is immobile, the bones of one leg having been shattered by a cannon ball, the other leg severely lacerated. He may be in one of his long fantasies about 'his lady'. Although in his thirtieth year, he is quite capable of daydreaming, as he admits, 'for two or three or four hours'. He had good models to draw upon 'as he was given to reading worldly and fictitious books usually called books of chivalry'. 'His lady' whom he describes as 'not a countess, nor a duchess, but her station was higher than any of these', is thought to have been the Princess Catalina, the younger sister of the Emperor Charles V. Her mother, the poor mad Queen Joanna could not bear to be separated from this her youngest and most beautiful child, who was therefore forced to share her mother's seclusion. In their austere palace her only relaxation was to watch from a high window the local children playing down below. An excellent focus, poor girl, for the quixotic reveries of the chivalrous Inigo, who may have glimpsed her three years before on her one, pitifully brief, visit to court.

Accomplished daydreamer though he certainly was, I doubt very much whether Inigo would have struck us as an abstracted introvert. He speaks of himself at this stage as 'given over to the vanities of the world'. These 'vanities' a later intimate was to list more bluntly as 'gaming, duelling and affairs with women', and adds the intriguing comment, 'this, however, was through force of habit'. The same source also gives him credit for more reputable activities. 'On several occasions he proved himself a man of great prudence and ingenuity in worldly affairs, especially in settling disputes'. What an extraordinary combination of qualities, those of the dreamer, the dissolute swaggerer, the responsible man of affairs. The gambling, duelling and womanising will disappear, but not the nerve, the will, the passionate disposition which fuelled them. The extremely sober, disciplined, resourceful, patient administrator of his last years will seem to have swallowed up both the dreamer and the buck. But it is not the gifts of the diplomat and administrator which pull men after you by the thousand and over a stretch of four centuries. They come in response to vision and passion.

Without his duties in the service of the Duke of Najera, without his boisterous and less seemly diversions, the long days of Inigo's convalescence palled. Even the most fertile imagination cannot provide its own entertainment indefinitely, so Inigo asked for his usual indulgence, a few chivalrous romances, to help him pass the sluggish hours. There were none, the rest of the Loyola family presumably not sharing his addiction, so they brought him 'a life of Christ and a book of the lives of the saints in Spanish'. In the absence of anything more to his taste Inigo settled down to read. In that moment St. Beuno's, together with a myriad of other Jesuit institutions both before and after it, was conceived.

As he read and re-read the story of Christ, the imagination that had warmed to the tales of Roland, Amadis and Lancelot caught fire. The deep suggestibility which led him to dream of imitating the legendary exploits of his heroes in the service of his 'lady' now prompted him to contemplate repeating the often equally legendary practices of the saints in the service of God. The uncalculating confidence, the ignorant fearlessness he had displayed in the late campaign now made these new goals seem quite attainable. Inigo refused to reckon up the odds. About Christian sanctity he had almost everything to learn . . . and he learned it. He was to achieve great sanctity and to evolve into one of the most important spiritual guides in the Church's history. He was to be granted quite extraordinary graces including the mystical illuminations of such Christian mysteries as the Trinity, creation and the presence of Christ in the eucharist. His ability to learn was quite extraordinary. I am not speaking of academic intelligence, although in this respect he was to show himself quite competent at the University of Paris, but of his powers of observation and his capacity for reflection upon what he had observed. He possessed the ability to patiently sift through experiences, to refrain from hurried assessment. He was willing to wait until certainty emerged. He remained ready to admit mistakes and to learn from them and yet, when he had given any matter due reflection, was firm in his decisions and resolute in their execution.

That the budding diplomat should be a careful observer of men and events is not surprising; that a gallant and a gamester should be accurately aware of his own emotions and able to review them dispassionately is not at all what one would expect. The outcome of this unusual combination was that just as Inigo had been able to reconcile opposed parties, so now was he able to monitor his interior self and reconcile the contradictions of his life in the pursuit of a single overriding purpose. This was to aim at sanctity, and to express that aim by journeying to Jerusalem on foot. Meanwhile, as he waited for his legs to gain strength, he re-read the books that had moved him so much, copied out extracts and, I am delighted to report, stargazed. 'The greatest consolation he received', he says of himself, 'was to look at the sky and the stars, which he often did for a long time'.

In his own account of the next sixteen years Inigo normally refers to himself as 'the pilgrim'. They were pilgrim years in several respects. He reached the Holy Land and would have stayed there indefinitely, had not the Franciscan superior with authority over all pilgrims, apprehensive of his indiscreet zeal, insisted on his return to Europe. Then began an academic pilgrimage which lasted eleven years, starting with the rudiments of Latin at Barcelona and finishing with theology in Paris. At a deeper level he continued his spiritual pilgrimage. This was the road on which he travelled furthest. Sometimes he was carried onward by mystical illumination; more often he plodded forward seeking counsel in confession, discussing spiritual things avidly and tirelessly whenever chance offered and, always observing himself, reflecting and assessing. In the externals of his life occurred a double transformation. Once well away from Loyola and his family and friends he had got himself up according to his own somewhat theatrical notion of what a pilgrim should look like, and then added to the effect by leaving his hair uncut and uncombed, his finger and toenails untrimmed. Two decades later we find him to outward appearance a perfectly presentable, if austere, cleric. A flamboyant courtier who commonly wore a bi-coloured suit and a cap with a jaunty feather, abruptly metamorphosed into a hippy-cum-tramp, slowly evolving into the unexceptionable, respectable priest, Ignatius had neither the conventional man's horror of the bizarre, nor the exhibitionist's fear of appearing ordinary.

Two other developments of this period are of importance in understanding the history of St. Beuno's. They are the beginnings of the Society of Jesus and the formation of the Spiritual Exercises.

The first was the result of an evolution more striking even than any already described. Inigo left his ancestral home to pursue holiness as a knight errant sought adventure and renown, riding off companionless on his solitary quest. Master Ignatius would die the leader and founder of a religious order already numbering almost a thousand men and destined to be the largest single order in the Church. Actually, he left home accompanied by his brother, but left him behind at their sister's house and made his way alone to Montserrat. There in the best chivalrous tradition he spent a night in vigil before the statue of Our Lady, donned not armour but a pilgrim's robe made to his own design. Then he journeyed to Manresa, a town some miles from Barcelona. In the course of a year his spiritual understanding developed hugely, thanks to a combination of divine illumination, guidance from well chosen confessors and unwearying self scrutiny. It has been said that at Manresa he evolved from 'knight penitent into knight apostolic', as he came to see that Christ does not call men and women to some giant-sized, inhuman penance, but rather he invites them to the humble, selfless, laborious continuance of Christ's own work. The relief of human need both of spirit and body. Did he also realise at this stage that he was also called to multiply his own individual effectiveness by inspiring others with the same ideals and by drawing some of them to work with him?

When he had returned from the Holy Land, settled at Barcelona and begun to study, three young men attached themselves to him and later accompanied him to the University of Alcala, where they were joined by a fourth. Obviously, Ignatius still believed in dressing the part, for the five all wore long grey garments which earned them the nickname 'sack wearers'. They conferred together often, lived very austerely, helped others generously and 'taught' i.e. spoke informally to groups and individuals about God, the soul, sin and the benefits of frequent confession and communion. Their common garb, and their zealous discourses, attracted the notice of the ecclesiastical authorities, who after conscientious enquiries forbade them to wear clothes of the same colour or to discuss matters of faith until they had completed four more years of study. The first instruction was promptly obeyed; the second found intolerable, so all five migrated to nearby Salamanca. Again they fell under suspicion, were investigated in the same painstaking way and this time were barred only from speaking of the difference between mortal and venial sin. Even this single handicap seemed to Ignatius too disabling and he decided to move once again, this time as far as Paris. The five agreed that he should go ahead to Paris and make arrangements for the others to follow. He went, and no-one followed. Without the immediate leadership of Ignatius the group lost its cohesion, each going his own way, one to a bishopric overseas, another to an edifying life as a Franciscan, the remaining two to less sanctified futures.

In Paris, seemingly no whit discouraged, Ignatius began again. Here he seemed to make better provision for his studies, which in Alcala seem to have taken a back seat, if, indeed, they were ever allowed anything more than standing room only. Yet he still found time to act as a one-man accommodation and social assistance bureau, and in conversation 'taught' as he had in Alcala, though, one presumes, with growing flexibility and expertise. The men who came together round him to form a stable group in Paris were of higher calibre and more durable material than their predecessors of Alcala. In August 1534 six of them joined him in a common vow, dedicating themselves to poverty in imitation of Christ and to sail to the Holy Land, there to work for the salvation of souls. Should they not be able to journey to the Holy Land, they would present themselves to the Pope and put themselves at his disposition. The precise terms of the vow are not recorded.

The summer of 1537 found the group, now numbering ten, waiting in Venice for a ship to Palestine. That year, for the first time in almost forty years, no ship sailed. War with the Turks, expected in the spring, finally broke out in the autumn, closing the seas indefinitely. Easter saw the group in Rome, having formally taken vows of poverty and chastity, received ordination and shown their apostolic mettle in a number of North Italian cities. Already they were identifying themselves to enquirers as the 'Company of Jesus'. During the spring months of 1539 they deliberated together concerning the nature and structure of their common enterprise. The document containing their conclusions finally received papal approval in September 1540.

In 1522 Inigo had expected, in the tradition of the knight errant, to fulfil his quest single-handed. The Jesuit, Ignatius and his companions decreed, would live and work as a member of a corporate body, as a part of a living organism, on which he would depend, and to which he would contribute. Inigo the page, the gallant, the pilgrim had always wanted to get the clothes right. The Jesuit was to have no distinctive garb whatever. Inigo had seen sanctity in terms of formidable penances. The Society of Jesus was to have no obligatory penances whatever. Nevertheless the questing chivalrous spirit of Inigo's heroes breathes through the whole structure of the Society. The Jesuit is in his own fashion a knight errant. He has no monastery to which he belongs; he belongs where the work is. He does not recite office communally, because his life must be flexible, and he himself as available as possible. He does not practise the physical austerities of Inigo at Manresa, but he is expected to have developed austerity of the spirit, practising poverty, cherishing simplicity, avoiding honours and power like the plague, welcoming humiliation and even persecution as intimations of intimacy with Christ condemned and crucified.

What did this revolutionary new order without its own habit or choral office do? They attempted to do whatever needed doing. At Ignatius's death three quarters of his priests were teaching in schools and colleges, a development of which the founding ten could have had no inkling. There were members at work in Asia, Africa and Latin America, their hair-raising adventures quite up to the standards of the bed-bound Inigo's daydreaming. Three members were nominated by the Pope to be his theologians at the Council of Trent in 1546, and there they met two confreres from Germany. Elsewhere in Europe Jesuits preached, heard confessions, gave spiritual direction and did battle with the ignorance of

Catholics and the errors of 'heretics'. Nor have things changed. Among the British Jesuits alongside whom I myself have studied, one was a 'peritus' (expert) at the Vatican Council; one became Director of the Vatican Observatory; several have taught at University level in Oxford, London, Harare and Japan. Others work in Guyana and Southern Africa. In Britain itself they have taught in schools and worked in parishes, published a few books and rather more articles, given 'retreats' and been chaplains in the universities, the armed forces and prisons. The only significant change since Ignatius's day is that whereas his men combatted 'heresy', my contemporaries include two distinguished ecumenists. We still try to do what needs to be done.

To walk round St. Beuno's, to inspect it from tower to cellars, is to understand little of its nature and purpose. Unless it can be seen against this background of four and a half centuries of constant activity, the story of St. Beuno's will make little sense. St Beuno's has the same roots as some of the most important teaching institutions in Rome, as so many hundreds of educational establishments in five continents, as the many imposing baroque churches in the great cities of Europe. The same foundations as innumerable mission churches and huts from Alaska to Madagascar, from South America to Hiroshima. The men behind all those buildings and many more, have all been inspired by Ignatius Loyola and formed by his Spiritual Exercises.

Concerning the Spiritual Exercises I shall be brief, partly from exigencies of space, chiefly from my own reluctance to talk about them. The Exercises are only to be understood by actually making them in the right dispositions under competent direction. Reading the printed book of 'The Spiritual Exercises' will shed about as much light on them as looking through the exam syllabuses in a university handbook will tell you about the experience of spending three years at a university. The book itself is little more than a syllabus for the director. The Exercises themselves are to do with seeing, appreciating, responding, choosing, willing and all in prayer. They are practical activities, not reading matter.

Inigo, the somewhat dissolute blade in his twenties, and Inigo, the deeply devout 'pilgrim' of his thirties believed the same Catholic doctrines. Why the difference in their lives? At Loyola, still more at Manresa, the religious truths, which in a sense he had held all his life, really penetrated his mind, his heart, his

imagination and determined his choices. Or should I perhaps say
that he penetrated into the depths of the doctrines and their
implications? Both, I think. Their truth sank into him; he im-
mersed himself in their reality. In the Exercises the exercitant
should repeat this experience. He (even in Ignatius's day it was
just as likely to be 'she') faces in prayer the great truths of
Christianity, opens his mind, opens his heart, is prepared to
scrutinise his whole self in the light of them, becomes willing to
redress any aspect of his life as prudent inspiration suggests.
It is far from being a purely intellectual process. The director
groans—silently!—when some very cerebral exercitant persists in
reducing the material to a satisfactory pattern of abstractions.
Equally, there must be no stampeding of the emotions by director
or exercitant. The director should be clear and brief, not rhetorical.
It is the truths themselves, the scripture passages in which they
are enshrined, the reflection of the exercitant, the prayerfulness in
which all must be done, but above all the impulse of grace which
must move the exercitant. Like the good teacher the director seeks
to 'eliminate' him or herself.

If the exercitant is concerned with traditional Christian truths,
what is so special about the Exercises? It is not the materials, not
the methods but the orchestration of the whole. The achievement
is in the arrangement of the material, the use of simple techniques
of prayer, the principles for judging what is happening, all taken
together. It is the sheer 'pointedness' of every exercise, of the
entire process. Ignatius knows exactly what he is doing at every
moment, and what he is hoping for and its relation to what has
gone before and will follow. Not that there is an iron pattern
which everyone must follow in exactly the same way. One aspect
of his genius was his ability to adapt to the individual, his mastery
of 'a lingering-out sweet skill'. Much of what he says in the
'Exercises' can strike one as no more than simple commonsense.
That is a considerable tribute to his shrewdness. He takes a truth
founded in accurate observation, carefully tested in application,
and enunciates it so unpretentiously that we think that we knew it
all along, that it appears self-evident. It is only when we ask
ourselves whether we and others are in the habit of acting in
accordance with it, that we realise that we have been taught
something valuable.

It is commonly agreed that the Exercises were for the most part put together during Ignatius's stay at Manresa, and that he continued to refine and add as late as his sojourn in Paris. Through them he hoped to communicate to others those of the insights he had received which were communicable, to evoke in their minds and imaginations the vision which now inspired his every action and to kindle in them the passion with which he responded to that vision. The structure of the Society of Jesus and all that it has ever achieved stems from the 'Exercises'. All its work in education and the mission field, in scholarship and publication is of less importance than its maintenance of the 'Exercises', the 'giving' of them to others and the effort to find the best way to deploy them in each generation.

St. Beuno's in its present phase as a Spiritual Exercises Centre is in the mainstream of the Ignatian tradition.

The Tower from the West

II

The Tower, Tyburn and transmigration

The tower of this chapter heading is not the modest affair which crowns St. Beuno's, but the rather larger, somewhat better known Tower of London, of which Shakespeare's doomed Prince of Wales says, 'I do not like the Tower of any place'. The English Jesuits of the sixteenth and seventeenth centuries would have agreed with him. It was in the Tower that they were liable, if captured, to be put to torture with the dreaded possibility that they might, when stretched in agony on the rack, give away information which could be used against their fellow priests or the lay people who had courageously sheltered them. Then, the Tower was often the last Station before the Calvary of Tyburn, the spot close to Marble Arch where traitors were hanged, disembowelled and quartered. At Tyburn a score of Jesuits perished publicly, ignominiously and very painfully. Five of them died together on the ill-omened or, from another point of view, blessed day of June 30th 1679.

Persecution, imprisonment and execution, all this was over long before the Jesuits arrived at St. Beuno's. Over, certainly, but not gone from the minds of the English Jesuits, for whom the heroic lives and deaths of their predecessors remained a matter of great pride and inspiration. In the vanguard of the first Jesuit mission to Elizabethan England in 1580, Edmund Campion had written, with a panache that would surely have delighted the knight-errant of Loyola, 'And touching our Society be it known to you that we have made a league cheerfully to carry the cross you shall lay upon us and never to despair your recovery, while we have a man left to enjoy your Tyburn, or to be racked with your torments or consumed with your prisons. The expense is reckoned, the enterprise is begun, it is of God, it cannot be withstood'. Within months of penning his 'Brag' Campion was being racked in the Tower, to be later tried and condemned and finally put to the ritual of hanging, drawing and quartering on December 1st 1581.

For a century and a half English Jesuits lived and died in an attempt to prove Campion's assertions true. More than seventy died on the scaffold, or in prison, or as the result of their sufferings in prison. To avoid capture they hid in carefully constructed priest-holes, or lurked for years in remote parts of some large Catholic household moving about in disguise, using aliases, sometimes several. A surprising number, when identified and captured managed to escape, either from the posse which was taking them to gaol or later from prison, even from the Tower itself.

A detailed, objective account of these events would have to point out that active persecution was sporadic, varying with the frequent changes of government policy and depending on the attitudes of local gentry and officials. It would point to the many Jesuits not executed but merely expelled, to the indulgent conditions which prevailed in some prisons where a jailer might be bribed to allow one to visit one's fellow Jesuits in another town. It would mention those who apostatised and men who had to be dismissed from the order. Perhaps, above all, it would point out that the Jesuits were always a minority among the priests who worked, risked and sometimes lost their lives to maintain the Catholic Faith among the English, Scots and the Welsh. None of these facts would the Victorian Jesuit have denied. He simply tended to lose sight of them through repeatedly hearing of the heroism of the Jesuit martyrs and the adventures of the missionary priests of former times. Men and events of which the Province had every right to be proud.

A Jesuit Province is the ordinary administrative unit of the Society and is directly responsible to the General. It was in 1623 that what had been the English Mission, and the English Vice-Province became a full Province. It had 248 members. I am sorry to say that although the territory of the Province included Wales, the Principality did not figure in its title. Whether this was due to Roman ignorance or to the usual indifference of the Anglo-Saxons to the distinctiveness of the Celtic fringe, I am not in a position to say. The Scots mission was a separate entity which died out in 1810. St. Beuno's was more than a decade old when some English Jesuits were sent to Glasgow and to Edinburgh. Both foundations flourished, Glasgow distinguishing itself by the many vocations it was to produce. These young men from Glasgow, together with

others from Edinburgh and elsewhere, found themselves joining
the English Province of the Society, an anomaly which was only
rectified recently in 1985 when the present General renamed us
'The British Province'. The change came about, I am glad to say,
at the Province's own request.

I often wonder about the Englishness of the English Jesuits
during the centuries of persecution. In 1593 the English Jesuits had
started a school at St. Omers in the Spanish Netherlands to which
faithful Catholic families might send their sons to be educated in
the old religion. Some of its pupils entered the Society joining the
noviceship, which had begun at Louvain in 1607 but eventually
settled down in 1627 at Watten only a few miles from St. Omers.
Philosophy and theology were studied at Liege, a small independent state of which the Prince Bishop was both the ecclesiastical
and temporal ruler. All three houses, St. Omers, Watten and Liege
obstinately maintained their English character though they were
surrounded by Flemings and Walloons, and were drawing sub-
sidies from the King of Spain, the King of France and the Elector
of Bavaria, and paying due deference to Spanish, and after 1678,
French officials.

Yet this was surely an Englishness which a Protestant fellow
countryman would have found more than a little alien. An English
Jesuit of, for instance, the eighteenth century might well have
come from a family whose Catholicism had kept them out of the
universities, the professions and government office and barred
them from national and local politics. In other words they lived
outside the mainstream of English national life. If a lad from such
a family spent his boyhood at St. Omers, passed into the novitiate
at St. Omers and was trained for the priesthood at Liege, how
much contact had he ever had with the normal English life of his
class? It seems to me that the English Jesuits lost on two fronts.
They were estranged, though quite unwillingly, from the mass of
their countrymen, while deliberately maintaining their distance
from the Flemings, Walloons etc. among whom they passed their
formative years.

I am making rather a meal of this point because it seems to me
to be a factor of considerable importance in English Jesuit history,
one which was still powerfully at work in my own younger days.
The English Province in which I was ordained was amazingly
insulated. Continental Jesuits had nothing to teach us because they

were foreigners, whose experience was *a priori* inapplicable to the English scene. Nor had other English Catholics anything to offer the members of the Church's largest, and, we took it, leading religious order. Certainly we did not expect to learn from the rest of England. We had the True Faith because we had refused to follow the path which Englishmen had for the most part taken, a path which was leading past Protestantism to religious indifference and sheer materialism. They were astray in matters religious, moral, social and political. It was for us to instruct them, not, of course, by entering into their thought patterns, but requiring them to adopt ours.

My statements are somewhat sweeping. There were exceptional individuals among us. Even official policy could sometimes be more open minded, as when in 1897 we began to send a few Jesuit students to Oxford University. Even this enlightened step seems to me to have made surprisingly little difference to our overall complacent mental isolation, which lasted into the sixties of this century.

As I leap from St. Omers and Liege in the eighteenth century to my own times the reader may well wonder whether I have lost sight of St. Beuno's. Not at all! I am, as a gunner would say, 'bracketing' it between the emigré Catholicism of penal times and the ghetto Catholicism of the first half of the twentieth century, asking myself where it fits between the two. First of all, I must admit, I should bring St. Beuno's into existence.

In the second half of the eighteenth century the English Jesuits suffered less at the hands of the Protestant English than from the hostility of Catholic monarchies. At this time the dominant groups in France, Spain, Portugal, Sicily and Naples were, for reasons utterly beyond the scope of this work, set to destroy the Society of Jesus, first in their own territories and then throughout the world. In 1762 the Paris Parlement forbade the continued existence of the Society in France and requisitioned all its property. This sweeping decree applied no less to the English Jesuits at St. Omers, which had been in French territory since 1678. It seems to have been the intention of the French authorities that the school be retained, possibly under the management of English diocesan priests. The English Jesuits literally stole a march on them. They moved out of the school in small groups with their pupils as though for a routine promenade and never returned. They made their way on foot and by barge and cart with what goods they had managed to smuggle out and could transport, to Bruges, a city at this time ruled from Vienna. Here the school valiantly set itself to continue its existence and teach its pupils, while the Jesuit novices set themselves up in Ghent.

There was worse to come. On August 16th 1773 Clement XIV, under pressure from the powers already listed, ordered the disbandment of the Society of Jesus. The 274 members of the English Province, in common with more than 22,000 of their brethren in four continents, found themselves no longer Jesuits. Providentially, the Prince Bishop of Liege decided to retain the house of studies where Jesuits had been preparing for the priesthood since 1614. He transformed it into the Liege Academy under his own authority, but with the former Jesuit Rector as its President. At Bruges the Austrian authorities, who had given the English Jesuits and their pupils a grudging welcome a dozen years before, now proved quite as hostile and predatory as the French. Again masters and boys took to road and water, this time to seek the haven of Liege. The complement of the Academy rose from 22 at the end of 1773 to 144 in 1776. It included boys, young laymen following higher studies, seminarists (I must not call them Jesuits) and the harassed staff.

If among the former Jesuits of Liege there was confusion and improvisation, among the hundred or so ex-Jesuits working in England and Wales there was equal bewilderment and rather less resource. While their work remained equally pressing, they found their links with the Society, with the Provincial, the local superior, and one another abruptly severed. Eventually some of them met in 1776 and established a central office to deal with their common interests, especially their financial affairs. At a second meeting in 1784 William Strickland, already President of Liege Academy, was elected to manage this central office. The meeting also agreed that there be 'a coalition and connexion of direction' between Mission and the Academy. By these two steps the English ex-Jesuits on the continent and in England were brought into an effective alliance in the common battle to stave off disintegration and demoralisation.

Only the ex-Jesuits in America drifted away. English Jesuits had been working in Maryland since 1634, and 1773 saw twenty-two members of the English Province facing more formidable problems than those perplexing their ex-brethren in Europe. One American born ex-Jesuit, John Carroll, was to become the first Catholic bishop in the United States. When the Society was restored the American Jesuits became a wholly independent unit, as behoved the citizens of the new Republic. Meanwhile, as the Maryland Jesuits went their own way, the ex-Jesuits of Liege and those working in England were brought together geographically by one of the great catalysts of European history, the French Revolution. In 1789 some of the Liegeois, inspired by the Fall of the Bastille, seized the great citadel which dominates their city, and put the Prince-Bishop to flight. In 1791 they lost control of the town to an Austrian army, which in turn fell back before a French Revolutionary Army, which was proving itself a very effective fighting force in spite of the wholesale defection of its aristocratic officer class. In the following spring the French retired to the great relief of the English staff of the Academy, as France and England were now formally at war. Even English phlegm was beginning to find this military seesaw somewhat unconducive to placid study and smooth academic routine, not to mention the danger from the increasingly fanatical French. When in 1794 French arms were again in the ascendant the community at Liege decided on yet another migration, this time to England itself, where they had been offered an old and vacant mansion at Stonyhurst in the Ribble valley, about fifteen miles from Preston. To South Lancashire, then, the ex-Jesuits with the few pupils that the war had left them made their way, by barge to Rotterdam, by ship to Hull, by barge again to Skipton and the last very weary twenty-five miles on foot. After two centuries the English Jesuit school and seminary were on English soil—except that the Jesuits were Jesuits no longer, and the products of their seminary could not join a Society which no longer existed!

Pity the poor Bishop, or more strictly the Vicar Apostolic of the Northern District, who now had in his territory a body of priests and students claiming to have brought with them from Liege the status of Pontifical Academy, an institution run by Jesuits who had no business to be such, and which would expect him to ordain as priests young men over whose training he had no control, and in whose subsequent employment he would have no voice! Pity still more the President, Fr. Marmaduke Stone, trying to run a school, a house of higher studies and a seminary altogether, in a mansion which had been unoccupied for half a century and was correspondingly dilapidated, while his canonical situation was even more full of holes, more cramped and unaccommodating than the semi-derelict building! He and his colleagues were somewhat heartened by a gleam of hope, born far away in Russia, and growing brighter. Back in 1773 the formidable Russian Empress Catherine II had refused to let the Jesuits in her Polish territories obey the Papal brief suppressing them. They, poor men, were caught between their reluctance to be suppressed, their obligations to obey the Pope and a natural unwillingness to defy their autocratic ruler. Fortunately for them, the Pope was almost as chary of offending Catherine as were her Jesuit subjects, and he connived at their continuance. In 1779, his successor, Pius VI, took the significant step of permitting them to accept novices. To the ex-Jesuits, at that date still at Liege, had come the heartening news that in at least one part of the world the Society still lived and had a future. Could they be part of that future? In 1801 Pius VII formally approved the position of the Russian Jesuits and went on to grant permission for them to accept members outside Russian territory. This the newly elected Russian General proceeded to do, and in 1803 Fr. Stone found himself Provincial over those English Jesuits who asked for readmission to the Society. He was also powered to accept novices. Thirty-three priests and two lay brothers renewed their vows as Jesuits, and twelve young men became novices at Hodder Place, a mile away from Stonyhurst. The English Province lived again.

The situation was now more heartening. It was also more complex. As President of Stonyhurst Fr. Stone had a staff some of whom had chosen to rejoin the Society, some of whom had not. As Provincial he was responsible for the Jesuits working in other parts of England and Wales and for former Jesuit property in the hands of ex-Jesuits. He worked under the further disadvantage that he and the Province which he administered, were not recognised by most of the Bishops or, more accurately, the Vicars Apostolic. Even the full restoration of the Society by Pius VII in 1814 failed to put an end to their objections and hesitations. Rome exasperatingly leaned one way and then the other in what was an intricate and protracted dispute, until in 1829 Leo XII declared unequivocally that Pius VII's restoration of the Society had full force in England and Wales.

The same year saw an event of far more concern to most Catholics than the rehabilitation of the English Jesuits. The dreams of generations of British Catholics had at last been realised with the lifting by Act of Parliament of almost all remaining legal penalties attached to the practice of Roman Catholicism. For the English Jesuits there was a fly in this excellent balm. One section of the Catholic Relief Act stated with regard to 'Jesuits and members of other religious orders' . . . that, 'it is expedient to make provision for the gradual suppression and final prohibition of the same'. The Act went on to state that no new member was to be admitted, and threatened offenders with banishment. These fire-breathing clauses were in fact nothing more than a smokescreen to reduce the opposition to the Bill of the more extreme anti-Catholic elements. The Jesuits in no way curtailed their operations; they did take precautions. The twelve intending novices of that year were all registered so that they would not be 'new members', whose admission was illegal. For years afterwards the Stonyhurst community listened to the monthly reading of the Rules with each of the three doors to the room guarded by a Jesuit. This obviously became something of a ritual with the guardianship of each particular door going with a certain office in the community. As late as 1870 the new member pronounced his vows in strict secrecy. Gerard Manley Hopkins describes this austere and clandestine rite, 'In a tiny chapel upstairs, lit by a skylight . . . Fr. Fitzsimon sat near a small table on which stood a crucifix, and we entered singly one after another, as though going to confession, and kneeling took our vows in secret . . . The Master of Novices merely answered Amen, took the written formula of the vows and the young religious withdrew'. Did they, I wonder, still consider it necessary to avoid any overt breach of a law which had never been enforced in forty years, or did they all get a faint thrill from the melodrama which linked them with the priestholes and secret meetings of the bygone heroic age?

Alongside this ceremonial circumspection went in other respects an almost blatant disregard for the huffings and puffings of the 1829 Act with its threat of 'gradual suppression and final prohibition'. In the very next year a new building came into service on the Stonyhurst site intended for the exclusive use of the Jesuit students. On what we might now call the Stonyhurst campus there coexisted from 1830 the school staff, the schoolboys, the

young men who stayed after the completion of their schooldays
for further study, the Jesuit students who were adding to their
knowledge of language and literature, those studying philosophy
and science in preparation for theology, and then the 'theologians'
proper, i.e. those engaged in the study of theology prior to
ordination. To these we must add their instructors and a number of lay brothers, while not forgetting the novices and the
preparatory school at Hodder Place. The opening of the new
'Seminary' building, later called St. Mary's Hall, relieved the
overcrowding only temporarily, and only partly removed the disadvantages of a miscellany of communities pursuing their different
ways of life in such proximity.

In 1844 a Provincial Congregation drew the attention of Fr.
General to this decidedly unsatisfactory situation. He in reply
insisted that an entirely separate establishment should be provided
for the theologians. I find it of interest that when a site for
the new theologate was under discussion some members of the
Province wished it to be near a large city. Others opposed the
suggestion on the grounds that country living was far cheaper and
very much healthier. This argument was to resurface in the course
of later decades, and while the reasons for an urban setting grew
in number and force, they continued to be met by this obstinate
concern for the young men's health. In consequence a growing
proportion of the Province, having been trained in a 'sweet
especial rural scene' or a succession of such, were then despatched
to the expanding schools and parishes of 'base and brickish'
London, Glasgow, Liverpool, Leeds and Preston, places undoubtedly 'bleared, smeared with toil', not to say smog-ridden, noisy
and in the nineteenth century subject to epidemics. It was a
setting for which the newly ordained Jesuit was both physically
and culturally ill-adapted.

In 1845 the unacceptable conditions at Stonyhurst were under-
lined and temporarily relieved by the uncompromising device of
sending all the theology students abroad. This was not what the
General or the Province wanted, and the urgent need to provide a
separate theologate in Britain (I almost wrote 'England'!) must
have been in the forefront of the Provincial's mind. It seems to
have been so when, perhaps in 1846, he paused on the crest of
Cwm Hill and seeing the Vale of Clwyd spread before him
exclaimed, 'Here I will build my theologate!'

The English Province of the Society had survived more than a century of active persecution in England and Wales, expulsion by the Bourbons, formal suppression by the Pope himself, flight before the armies of the Revolution and more recently the obstructionism of the Vicars Apostolic. When the 'theologians' arrived in North Wales they brought as it were in their baggage a noble tradition of courage, endurance and hope against the odds.

The Rock Chapel

III

Let us build a tower

The full quotation reads: 'Come let us build ourselves a city, and a tower with its top in the heavens'. Fr. Randal Lythgoe was without the hubris of the men of Babel, but showed himself to be almost their equal in enterprise and far more effective in execution. The institutions he founded were long lived and the buildings he begat still stand. In 1841 the English Province consisted of Stonyhurst with its conglomeration of communities, and numerous missions throughout the country, most of them managed by a single priest. Fr. Lythgoe, becoming Provincial in that year, was soon hauling his colleagues out of their rut and launching them on a series of new enterprises. In 1842 he started a second boarding school at Mount St. Mary's, Spinkhill, Derbyshire, and in the same year began a day school in Liverpool, St. Francis Xavier's College, where I myself was destined to become a pupil in the school's tenth decade. In 1845 he opened a college in Malta which, with one hiatus of some years, was to survive into the twentieth century. He enlarged the buildings at Stonyhurst and greatly improved their appearance, adding the West Wing and the Infirmary building. He laid the foundations of Farm Street, London, the Province's best known church, and built other churches, some of them edifices of distinction, in Liverpool, Great Yarmouth, Clitheroe and Tunbridge Wells. As Provincial he was making a routine visitation of the Jesuit parish at Holywell when he decided to go over to a farm near Tremeirchion, a property which the Province seems to have owned since 1662. It was on this journey that he breasted Cwm Hill, saw our valley, and, according to legend, thumped his knee and made his celebrated declaration of intent.

Fr. Lythgoe was bringing his students into what might be for them alien territory, but was in fact quite rich with Jesuit associations. Jesuits had worked in North Wales from early times and some members of the Province had been born there. Fr. John Bennett (1548(?)-1625) was born near Holywell, educated at St. Asaph and worked as a diocesan priest in Wales 'especially the north parts thereof'. He was arrested in 1582, imprisoned in Flint Castle, taken to Ludlow for torture and then banished. This enforced sojourn on the continent he used to join the Society of Jesus. He then returned to Britain and his work in North Wales, but died in London, having volunteered to tend the plague victims of the capital. Thomas Pennant (1579-1638), a native of Flintshire, who had been a schoolboy at Hawarden, worked and died in Wales. Talacre on the mouth of the Dee, some eight miles from St. Beuno's, was the seat of the obstinately Catholic family of Mostyn, which gave three of its members to the Society. John (1657-1721) worked mostly in South Lancashire. His brother Andrew served mostly in Worcestershire. Their nephew Piers (1687-1735), who inherited the baronetcy in 1720, like John worked in Lancashire.

Hugh Owen (1615-86) was born in Anglesey and served in North Wales. He survived the hysterical persecution stirred up by Titus Oates in 1678, when two other Welsh Jesuits perished. One, David Lewis, was hanged at Usk; the other, Philip Evans, who when in prison borrowed the governor's harp to accompany his own singing, was executed at Cardiff. Hugh evaded capture, lived another eight years and died by falling from his horse at the age of seventy-one. Humphrey Evans, also of Carnarvonshire, worked as a priest for fifty-three years and was Superior of the Mission, first in South Wales and then in the North. The frenzy of the year 1678 found him eighty years old, bedridden, without the use of his limbs or the power of speech. The investigators hauled him out of bed on Christmas morning, bawled at him in the hopes of getting an answer and threatened him with their muskets. Three months later, to nobody's surprise he died.

William Morgan (1623-89) had enough adventures for three men. Born in Flintshire, educated at Westminster Grammar School, he went to Cambridge, but on the outbreak of the Civil War quit the University to fight, like so many Welshmen, in defence of his King. He was taken prisoner at the battle of Naseby, imprisoned for some months then banished. Abroad he joined an English unit in the Spanish army, became a Catholic, went to Rome to study for the priesthood and in 1651 joined the Society. Reviving the academic capacity he had shown at Westminster, he held a number of teaching posts in the seminaries of Rome before being sent to the English Province seminary at Liege as 'Professor of Philosophy, Hebrew etc.' (I like the 'etc.'). In 1672 he returned to his native North Wales, became the local Superior, was specially targeted by the Oates investigation but managed to escape to the continent. At this point the English mission was a shambles. Eight men, the Provincial among them, had been executed, several others had died in prison or as a result of imprisonment and the rest were either doing their best to hide or had already fled to the continent. The Rector of the seminary at Liege was appointed to the vacant office of Provincial and made Fr. Morgan his Socius (Assistant). The new Provincial's first need was for information, so the even newer Socius was asked to carry out a reconnaissance of the shattered mission and report back. Morgan courageously stepped back into the lion's den, was arrested, but later, in the milder climate of 1683, released. Returning, no doubt with relief, to the continent, he became Rector of the English College, Rome, and in 1689 was appointed to the post of Provincial. Unfortunately the Province was never to experience the leadership of this many-sided man as his appointment was followed by his death five weeks later. I like to think of the shade of that Welsh Provincial-Of-Five-Weeks present on Cwm Hill, and chuckling with delight as his thirtieth successor in office decided that priests of the English Province would in future learn their theology not only in Wales, but in the country of Morgan's own birth. (Note: When St. Beuno's was built it stood in the County of Flintshire. By the rearrangements of 1974 it found itself in the newly created, agreeably named county of Clwyd).

Holywell, from which Fr. Lythgoe had set out on that historic day, has a special place in the religious history not only of Wales, but of England also. Its legend tells of Winefrid, a Christian maid, fleeing from the lustful advances of Caradoc, the son of a local chieftain, being pursued by him, overtaken and beheaded. Both her life and her head were miraculously restored to her by her uncle St. Beuno, so that she lived for many years afterwards, a dedicated and saintly nun in a far mountain valley. From the spot where her severed head had fallen there gushed a spring with healing powers, which proved one of the most popular places of pilgrimage in Britain.

'Here to this holy well shall pilgrimages be,
And not from purple Wales only, nor from elmy England,
But from beyond the seas, Erin, France and Flanders,
everywhere,

Pilgrims, still pilgrims, more pilgrims, still more poor pilgrims.' Not vintage Hopkins! Nor were all the pilgrims poor. To the shrine of Holywell Henry V came on foot the year after Agincourt, walking all the way from Shrewsbury to pay his respects to St. Winefrid. Margaret Beaufort, the mother of Henry VII enriched the shrine with a fine chapel. Even after the Reformation the pilgrims continued to come, causing the local authorities to send an alarmed report to Charles I's Privy Council. Dr. Johnson passed by a century and a half later and observed people bathing in the still hallowed waters.

When in 1670 the Jesuits working in the northern areas of Wales were organised into the administrative unit so misleadingly called a 'residence', it was given the title of The Residence of St. Winefrid, and its principal base was at Holywell. Here the Society had acquired a piece of property in 1669. James II, the Catholic Stuart, like his Plantagenet ancestor came to pray at the shrine, and in 1687 his consort Maria gave money for the restoration of the chapel, putting the work in the hands of the Jesuits. Sadly for his Catholic subjects the following year saw James II deposed and in exile. The chapel promptly reverted to secular use and the Jesuit Superior spent nine months in gaol. The hiccup of the Glorious Revolution over, the Jesuits resumed their service of the local Catholics and the visiting pilgrims, treating a raid by Dragoons in 1718 and even the period of the suppression of the Society as inconveniences of varying duration.

In 1862 Francis Lythgoe, Randal's cousin, came to Holywell as a newly ordained priest and it is recorded that after a few years residence he was preaching regularly in Welsh. Randal apparently shared his cousin's respect for things Welsh, giving his new theologate the title of St. Beuno's College. Beuno, whom we have met giving such effective first aid to his decapitated niece, seems to have been almost as important in the religious history of North Wales as the national patron, St. David, was in the South. The actual events of his life, lived probably in the late sixth century, are so overlaid with legend as to be irrecoverable. Yet it is clear from the number of churches dedicated to him, and from the number of wells and springs associated with him that he was a man of stature and influence. He was honoured in Eastern Wales, in our own Clwyd, in Anglesey and especially in the Lleyn peninsula. It is, I think, greatly to the credit of Fr. Lythgoe, that more than a century before the birth of that graceless word 'inculturation' he should have named his seminary after an eminent Welsh saint and the one most honoured in all North Wales. A couple of decades later and Tremeirchion might well have had a College of the Sacred Heart or the Immaculate Conception, with none of the inmates adverting to the insensitivity of such alien and aggressively post-Reformation nomenclature. I am always grateful that the house was built before British Catholicism surrendered to the cultural imperialism of Ultramontanism with its disregard for history and its obtuse conviction that Catholic unity implies a blanket uniformity.

The farm which Fr. Lythgoe had been on his way to visit had an outlying field which looked a suitable site, and he came to inspect it in the company of two other priests and the brother of one of them, a physician. The doctor was there presumably to pass professional judgement on the healthiness of the location. He must have declared it salubrious, as an architect was engaged, plans drawn up and approved and the work launched. One obstacle according to an unattributed handwritten Latin account was the refusal of local landowners to supply sand or stone for the erection of a Papist building. Providentially, further inspection of the site unearthed a good deal of sand and usable stone on the site itself together with an adequate water supply. The same anonymous Latinist goes on to describe the Welsh as resentful, envious, materialistic and happy to defraud the English and also as having 'mores pessimi' (atrocious morals). No 'inculturation' there, but a sad amalgam of Anglo-Saxon superiority and Catholic bigotry. These regrettable factors do not however disqualify him as a chronicler in the matter of sand, stone supplies and the availability of water!

The architect chosen for the new theologate was Joseph Aloysius Hansom, a Catholic who had demonstrated his virtuosity by designing Birmingham Town Hall in 1831 and a Patent Safety Cab three years later. It is almost a ritual with me to say, 'The house was designed by Hansom of the hansom cab', while asking teacher-like how many of my hearers know what a hansom cab was like, or have even heard of one before. Hansom provided a solid, square building with Neo-Gothic features. In using the Neo-Gothic style he was in the fashion, for the Romantic movement had made the pseudo-mediaeval aesthetically acceptable and the ecclesiasticism of the Oxford Movement hallowed it with a touch of spurious sanctification. Without its tower, the angel roof in the chapel and its Gothic finials the building would indeed be dull, yet I can only wonder whether the study of Neoscholastic theology (of which more anon) in a Neo-Gothic building, in a rural setting was a very effective preparation for the evangelisation of London, Glasgow and Liverpool.

Hansom's St. Beuno's enclosed a square garden on the west side of which there was a basement gallery containing the Recreation Room, a schoolroom (their word for it), two private rooms and the Entrance Hall. On the floor above was the Library, which looks both inside and out as though it were a chapel, the Rector's room and a 'Stranger's' Room. On the south side, the tallest side, rising even a little higher than the Tower, were three galleries which housed the 'professors' and the students. On the north side was the quite monastic refectory or dining room with its pulpit for the reader. Meals were usually silent in the sense that the diners did not talk, but were solemnly read to from some suitably edifying volume. Sometimes a practice sermon from one of the students was substituted for the reading, which enables me to say to some stolid visitor, 'That is the pulpit where Gerard Manley Hopkins and I gave our practice sermons', mischievously suppressing the fact that we did so some seventy years apart. Between the refectory and the tall south side runs a modest block with only two floors and a handful of rooms, some of which were earmarked for the infirmary. That sounds as though someone anticipated a very frail bunch of students or a series of epidemics, whereas the defects of contemporary medicine and the lack of hospital facilities required some sensible provision for sickness, accidents and death. So there was an infirmarian, at least in theory, a dispensary and a room or two set aside for the sick. I suspect from the house lists that there was often no infirmarian available, and that when there was pressure on room space the sick rooms were snapped up for ordinary accommodation. The rooms in this area have their windows looking into the enclosed garden while the rooms on the south and west look outward from the building. Perhaps the rooms looking into the garden were considered less exposed and therefore warmer, and so more suitable for the sick.

From this northern side the chapel projected at right angles and

on straight into the hillside. The early history of the chapel is
irritatingly obscure. It certainly was not ready when the students
arrived and the first academic year began. For a time mass was
said in a room on the Chapel Gallery (the first floor of the south
side), then in the Library. The condition of the chapel I find hard
to imagine. An early, but not contemporary, description runs,
'The floor was a staircase, descending from high altar (an ugly
thing) . . . a fall of about twelve feet or more, or one foot to every
yard'. 'All the arches which are now to be seen were blocked
up . . . A hideous wooden gallery projected from that end wall'.
In 1852 the Rector, Fr. Etheridge with the assistance of a student,
Richard Vaughan, took the matter in hand most effectively. The
floor was levelled, the arches on the right opened up and the
chapel extended to take four side altars. The tribune (choir loft)
was added and eight stained-glass windows put in. One such
window, that depicting St. Beuno, is worth a second look, not for
any artistic merit but because the saint is holding St. Beuno's on
his arm, and it is the original building without its later extension
to the north of the Tower. St. Beuno's at that stage, I think, must
have looked as though a minor monastery, a college building and
a small fort had fused together into a tight defensive square
against the gales which blow from the Irish Sea . . . or against the
winds of change?

Sometimes when one is conducting a visitor through the house
we arrive at the chapel and the visitor drops to his or her knees
for a moment's prayer. So I, arriving in this narrative at the chapel
redressed by Fr. Etheridge to a more dexterous order, am con-
strained to pause, the reader, I hope, alongside me.

'You are here to kneel
Where prayer has been valid'.

Indeed it has. Here for three quarters of a century the
'theologians' of the English Province gathered in formal, communal
worship or 'dropped in' singly for their private devotions.
Annually in this chapel, after what seemed a lifetime of
waiting—'a Jesuit is ordained as a reward for a wellspent life'—the
Third Year became priests of the Church and offered mass for the
first time. These prayer-soaked stones have witnessed the children
of the neighbourhood collected for confirmation when the bishop
decided to confer two sacraments during one visit; they have
watched the Tertians praying, perhaps rather impatiently, as they

waited out their last year of formation; they have listened to the nervously pronounced First Vows of novices. These same stones have been hallowed by the long, unhurried prayers of old Jesuits, their years of labour over, the denarius, which it takes an eternity to spend, still to be paid them; they have been blessed by the quick, opportunist orisons of the lay brothers inserted between chores. They have seen the local Catholics dutifully come to mass, along with occasional holiday makers looking about them uncertainly, not sure what sort of church they have come to.

For more than a century the chapel saw, with the exception of local Catholics, only Jesuits. Here they prayed as they prepared to go hence and work alongside other priests, to minister to nuns and laity, to engage in controversy with other Christians. These days British Jesuits are often an insignificant minority in the chapel, which sees at mass and single meditation diocesan priests, members of very many congregations of both men and women, and lay people with in each category members of other communions. Of the Jesuit students who assembled in this chapel perhaps a fifth, perhaps even every fourth, was destined to work in Africa, the Caribbean or elsewhere overseas. The chapel now warms to the presence of people from every continent and from every region with the exception of Eastern Europe and Russia. The whole situation seems to have been reversed in every particular as though the building alone gave a semblance, and that misleading, of continuity. This impression is however misleading. The Jesuit student was here because Ignatian inspiration had called him, held him and would continue to motivate him. The person who now occupies his room and worships where he worshipped has come to make or to learn about the Ignatian Exercises or in some way to draw upon the inspiration they provide. In a profound sense, 'Plus ca change, plus c'est la même chose'.

Now my over-ready strictures on Ultramontanism, my supercilious comments on the cult of the Neo-Gothic, turn sour upon my tongue. Not that they are untrue: I could defend each word. They came so easily to my pen, whereas to focus on a hundred years and forty of worship and summarise it even inadequately, to sketch the evolution of the influence of the Exercises even in an extremely foreshortened form has been so taxing. I find myself abashed and chastened, a salutary effect perhaps of our short visit to the chapel.

IV

He built a watchtower

Let me quote more at length:
'My beloved had a vineyard on a very fertile hill.
He digged it and cleared it of stones, and planted it with
choice vines;
He built a watchtower in the midst of it.'
Fr. Lythgoe, although shying perhaps at the word 'beloved',
would probably have liked the comparison with a vineyard. The
theologate he had planted on a not so fertile Welsh hillside was
close to his heart. As we have seen, he had started three new
colleges in a Province which previously had but one, and extended
some of its other commitments at a time when he had less than
ninety priests in all at his disposition. The success of these spirited
ventures now depended on good annual yield from this new
vineyard. At the completion of his term of office on January 1st
1848 he took personal charge of the clearing and planting on the
side of Moel Maenefa and was there to greet the first batch of
students on their arrival. They had come from Stonyhurst to
Liverpool and then taken a paddle steamer to Mostyn on the
estuary of the Dee, and presumably travelled the last eight miles
or so in some horse-drawn conveyance.

The formal opening took place on October 30th., Fr. John
Etheridge being installed as Rector of a community consisting of
himself, a Minister (Bursar), five professors (lecturers), twenty
scholastics (students) and eight laybrothers. I think that the first
response of a present day member of the British Province might be
to exclaim nostalgically and wistfully at that generous complement
of brothers. A teacher might envy the 'professors' their pupil ratio,
but that is to forget that they had to handle the full range of
theological study both academic and pastoral. They had to initiate
their pupils into the world of theological scholarship; they had also
to turn them into competent, sufficiently down to earth, pastoral
priests. The tension between those two aims was, it seems to me as
a student, still not wholly resolved even a century later. However

I may not be making sufficient allowance for the fact that the twentieth century made more stringent demands in both areas. Coming from Liverpool to Mr. Hansom's semi-monastic building amid the Welsh hills, those twenty students (some sources say that there were only eighteen at the opening) must have had the air of men reviving the ancient ascetic practice of withdrawing from the world and fleeing the cities of men. Yet that building had been built for only one reason, to prepare them to engage with the world and to serve the cities of men. How humiliatingly easy it is for me, trying to recreate in my imagination those first days of St. Beuno's, to lose sight of the world beyond the Dee and still more that beyond the Channel. The date 1848 should resonate loudly in the mind of anyone with any knowledge of nineteenth century history. It was a year packed with dramatic events. February of that year saw the barricades going up in Paris, Louis Philippe in flight and France once more a republic. In March an uprising of the Viennese toppled Prince Metternich, the man who had tried to organise all the governments of Europe to co-operate in making such events impossible. In Northern Italy an ill-armed populace managed to drive the Austrian garrisons out of most of Lombardy and Venetia. In Berlin the citizens seized control of the city and were promised radical constitutional changes, and there were similar revolts with similar results in most of the other kingdoms and principalities into which Germany was still divided. Palermo in Sicily and Naples on the mainland had both erupted even before the Parisians had started to arm.

The anonymous Latinist whom I took to task in the last chapter for his cantankerous comments on the Welsh was able to sum up the whole insurrectionary scenario in a single dismissive line: 'nefanda illa coniuratio quae anno 1848 totam Europam evertit', i.e. 'that unspeakable conspiracy which in 1848-9 turned all Europe upside down'. Of course he is wrong again. The 'revolution' did affect almost all of Europe, but it was certainly not the achievement of a single conspiracy or of one carefully orchestrated alliance. The middle classes were concerned with civil liberties and constitutions; the industrial workers and peasants fought for their economic and social betterment; North Italians wanted independence of Austria, Hungarians and Czechs more autonomy, German patriots national unity. The forces at work were so different in the different countries, so disparate at times even in the same country as often to finish up not merely disunited, but even in open conflict.

What did the newly gathered community of St. Beuno's think of these events which looked like turning the continent upside down? Were they even aware of them? Aware, certainly, and their attitude almost certainly that of my unidentified Latin chronicler. Of the five men gathered to teach them two had been driven out of their native Switzerland and two others forced to leave Rome, so the accounts retailed at St. Beuno's were partly first hand, undoubtedly lively and wholly partisan. Already, months before the opening of St. Beuno's, the entire Province had been shocked to hear that Fr. Roothaan, the General, had fled Rome, urged thereto by the Pope himself, and was managing the affairs of the harassed Society as best he could from Marseilles. Before St. Beuno's had celebrated its first Christmas Count Rossi, the Pope's liberal, reforming minister would be assassinated and the Pope, powerless and defenceless, would be a refugee in Gaeta. It was not a situation to engender nuanced and qualified judgements. It would have been a remarkable Jesuit seminarist who in 1848 did not deplore wholeheartedly the successes of the revolutionaries, and rejoice equally wholeheartedly when 'sooner or later, in every country and in every respect the revolution encountered failure'.

He rejoiced too soon. The tide had gone out; it would certainly return. The flood waters of nationalism, the political and social groundswell from major economic changes, would inevitably carry away the structures of the ancient regime. Wherever the Church with its organisation and personnel was seen as part of an oppressive and anachronistic framework the tidal waves would not spare it. In France, twenty years before, the imaginative Lamennais had wanted the Church to go with the tide: 'God and liberty—unite them!' His sweeping programme to make liberalism Catholic found no effective support in Rome and was condemned in the encyclical 'Mirari Vos' of 1832. Fr. Roothaan had then demanded from every Jesuit teacher of philosophy an explicit retraction of whatever degree of approval they might have expressed of Lamennais' system. At a later date, in 1847 an Italian Jesuit, d'Azeglio, had urged, much more circumspectly than Lamennais, the possibility of a reconciliation between the Church and liberalism; 'We should not only not speak unfavourably about this trend (liberalism), but show in a positive way that, once its anti-Christian hostility has ceased, our resistance also ceases'. Fr. Roothaan had commented quite moderately, "I neither approve the adulation of some for princes nor the exaggerated aversion of others for all that pertains to liberalism. But if one considers that, in substance, liberalism tends of its nature towards liberty, or rather towards a freedom from any and every kind of restraint, and that up to the present its fruits in those regimes that have a constitution are bitter rather than not, (I am speaking of those countries which until recent times have been monarchical), I do not wonder that only with difficulty can one become a partisan of it". In 1848, as we have seen, Fr. Roothaan had to digest some very sour fruit forced on him by the revolutionaries, including threats of assassination and twenty five weary months of exile. After that the teeth of his sons would be set on edge for some generations.

It is because of those later generations that I have dwelt on the almost Wagnerian continental accompaniment to the innocuous, clerical, rustic idyll of the opening of St. Beuno's. Admittedly, the mutual suspicion and reciprocated fear between liberal and churchman began before 1848. It can be traced at least as far back as the ideologues of the 'Enlightenment' in the eighteenth century, of whom the most extreme proposed to 'strangle the last aristocrat with the bowels of the last priest'. It can be traced through the story of the French Revolution, the kidnapping of Pius VII by Napoleon and the revolts of 1830. Then 1848 and the two year exile of the General confirmed the English Jesuits' antipathy to continental liberals and reformers, an attitude which was to receive further reinforcement throughout the rest of the century. 'In 1859, 1860 and 1870 the Society was dispersed in Italy, in 1868 expelled from Spain, in 1872 from Germany; in 1880 from France'. If these events seemed remote when first reported at St. Beuno's, they certainly ceased to be so when foreign scholastics sought asylum at St. Beuno's, as did a large number of Italians in the wake of 1870. In 1873 the entire German theologate settled at Ditton Hall near Widnes, and remained till 1895. They were a part of that forced exodus which in 1875 brought five German nuns in the Deutschland 'American-outward-bound' to be 'sealed in wild waters' on the Kentish Knock. In the year 1881 the scholastics of the Lyons Province came in a body to Mold, a dozen miles from St. Beuno's. They settled in the 'Old Prison', which with Gallic tact they christened 'St. David's College', and remained there till 1897. For a period of about fourteen years a Tremeirchion crow, curious to compare the Jesuit theologians of Britain, Germany and France, could have fitted his researches into a triangular trip of about seventy miles. Meanwhile, the General, Fr. Beckx, managed the affairs of the Society from Florence instead of Rome, which he had had to leave in 1873 and to which he was unable to return. It was 1895 and two generals later that the Society's central office moved back to Rome after an absence of twenty-two years, which makes Fr. Roothaan's exile of twenty-five months seem but a brief intermission.

'On a pastoral forehead of Wales
I was under a roof here, I was at rest,
And they the prey of the gales.'

Hopkins' lines about himself and the five German nuns, their 'doom to be drowned', could have been aptly quoted by any imaginative nineteenth century Jesuit student contrasting his own uneventful days with those of his continental brethren, as yet another Province faced expropriation and exile. What was the effect, I wonder, on the young English Jesuit of this continental backcloth? I much regret that I have no direct evidence on the point and can only speculate on the consequences of this surely not unimportant part of his mental horizon. I would link it with the fact that every evening at supper he listened to an extract from the 'Menology', which commemorated those members of the Province who had distinguished themselves in the heroic days when the lot of the English Province had also been one of persecution and exile. Did he feel uncomfortable and rather feeble to be living so tame, so comfortable, if circumscribed, a life in comparison with the lives of his British predecessors and his continental contemporaries? Perhaps I am projecting onto those Victorian Jesuits the effect on myself of living safely 'under a roof here', when my school contemporaries were being shot down over Germany and dying in North Africa and Burma.

I also wonder whether, while feeling somewhat inferior to his persecuted continental brethren, he was also conscious of the superiority of being British, of belonging to a nation that not only led the world in commerce, industry, naval power and overseas possessions, but had outgrown civil war, revolution and the violent clash of political and religious differences. I have no doubt at all that the whole situation helped to produce an unspoken conviction of the English Jesuits of the first half of the twentieth century that we had nothing to learn from continental Jesuits, the context in which we lived and worked being, in our own eyes, unique. I am similarly convinced that the expulsions and confiscations experienced by foreign Jesuits helped to confirm the English Jesuits in what we would now call their right wing sympathies. These attitudes would persist into the twentieth century, to be confirmed by the Russian Revolution and the Spanish civil war. It was an unusual and independent- minded member of the Province who in the first half of this century saw things political from a different standpoint.

In Britain itself, the land where the St. Beuno's students of 1848 had been born and in which they expected to work and die, 1848 was not a year of revolution, but rather the year when revolution was avoided. In that year the Chartists, stimulated by the success of the Paris rising of February, called a national convention for April. At it they decided to present once more their petition to Parliament for the implementation of their famous Charter. This document, first published in 1838, already rejected by Parliament in 1839 and 1842, called for a total reform of the parliamentary system, including such radical demands as annual parliaments, universal male suffrage and the payment of members of the House of Commons. The government deployed its troops, police and special constables effectively but unprovocatively. The great procession to escort the petition was prohibited and the demonstrators quietly dispersed. Nor was there any appreciable disturbance in the provinces.

If, in spite of considerable political dissatisfaction and economic distress the country did not erupt in 1848, it was not because Britain was inert or stagnant. The impression left on one by a survey of the period is of accelerating movement. Britain was changing faster than ever before in its history. The population was increasing at an unprecedented rate. In 1821 the population of England and Wales was 12,000,000; in 1851 18,000,000. As thirty was a common age for starting at St. Beuno's, there were three people in Britain as the Jesuit scholastic started theology, for every two at the time of his birth. The population was not only growing, it was moving, chiefly from the countryside to the town. In London in 1851 half the inhabitants had been born elsewhere; in

Glasgow, Liverpool and Manchester three out of every four. One person in ten in Britain had been born in Ireland. Between 1841 and 1851 more than a million and a half Britons emigrated. People and things were moving about more, and usually faster. By 1848 the main structure of the railway system had been established and was constantly being added to. The Chester to Bangor line, passing along our coast, was opened in 1848 and the line through the valley to Ruthin in 1858. From that time it became normal to come to St. Beuno's, or leave it, via St. Asaph station. Between 1827 and 1848 the total tonnage of British shipping almost doubled. In 1850 almost 60% of the world's ocean-going tonnage was British, and the volume of shipping in and out of British ports, excluding the coastal trade, doubled in the decade preceding 1847. The steamship, still expensive to build, was crossing the Atlantic in half the time taken by the fastest sailing vessels.

From 1840, thanks to Sir Rowland Hill, letters and packages were travelling faster, cheaper and in ever mounting numbers. In 1844 the first telegraph line in England was installed between Paddington and Slough and in 1851 the first cable to the continent was laid. The output of coal almost doubled between 1836 and 1851; the output of iron more than trebled between 1830 and 1850. By 1850 Britain had become 'the workshop of the world' and its principal shipper and trader. Its technical triumphs, its scientific progress, the projects it had ready for further development, all these were confidently celebrated in the Great Exhibition of 1851.

The Catholic community was changing with the nation of which it was a part. It too was growing and moving. The English Catholics were taking part in the general move from the countryside to the towns, and the Irish were coming over the sea. Their numbers were certainly increasing. It is calculated that in 1770 there were 80,000 Catholics; in 1850 three quarters of a million. This expansion was not due solely to the Irish influx. In the cities and towns of South Lancashire the number of Catholics had increased fourfold in half a century. The Irish immigration was certainly large. In Liverpool, Manchester and Preston by 1851 the Irish appear to predominate over the English Catholics in the proportion of three to one. Both the movement from the countryside to the town and that from Ireland changed the structure of the Catholic community. The Catholic aristocracy and particularly the landed gentry became much less important in

Catholic affairs. The clergy were no longer so dependent on their support and influence; the congregation no longer consisted of their tenants, employees and other people conscious of their standing. In consequence, the leadership of the Catholic community tended to become concentrated in the hands of the clergy, so that later in the century they would come to regard their monopoly as divinely instituted. 'In the Church of God' Cardinal Manning would smugly declare, 'there is no House of Commons'. In 1848 Manning was still an Anglican archdeacon and would remain so for another three years. Newman on the other hand had left the Anglican Communion three years before St. Beuno's opened. Newman and Manning are the most illustrious representatives of another new and most valuable element in the Catholic Church in England, those who had come to it via the 'Oxford Movement'. Of twenty-one English scholastics at St. Beuno's in 1850 four were former Oxford men.

The young men at St. Beuno's could not be bishops in their own country, and none of them ever made it to Cardinal. They would still have to shoulder a good deal of responsibility in a growing and changing Church in a bustling, evolving Britain forever producing more goods and new problems. At first glance St. Beuno's, its architecture semi-monastic, its centuries-old religious and academic routines unhurried, its relaxations gentlemanly and rural, would seem to exist in another dimension. This is to forget its founder. Fr. Lythgoe, innovative, resolute, bold to the point of gambling, is a typical Victorian entrepreneur. St. Beuno's was a new venture and with the resources at his disposal an uncertain one. As we have seen, four of his small lecturing staff were temporary refugees. He was investing in new schools, in bigger churches and he had produced a new theologate. He had set up a new factory to extend his business, his business being the production and deployment of adequately trained Jesuits. Fr. Lythgoe was a man of his time.Whether the religious discipline of the new theologate and its academic methods, over neither of which Fr. Lythgoe had jurisdiction, best fitted a man for re-entry into 'the workshop of the world' is quite another matter.

Two other events demand to be noticed before we leave the year 1848. In the autumn of 1845 the potato blight appeared in Ireland. In 1846 it had destroyed the potato crop, or more accurately three quarters of it, by July. By 1851, in the words of the census commissioners, 'very nearly one million' Irish people had died, some by starvation, others from the epidemics which, supervening on near-starvation, killed more people in the wake of the famine than hunger had during it. Another million emigrated during the same half decade, and a further million in the ten years after that. Manning was to say drily that, having left the Church of England, he then found himself 'working for the Irish occupation of England'. Many of the young Englishmen at St. Beuno's would before long have good reason to feel the same way.

Lastly, an event the importance of which requires no comment from me: in February, 1848, there was published in London a joint work composed by Karl Marx and Friedrich Engels. They entitled it 'The Communist Manifesto'.

V

A Tower . . . firmly set

From 1848 until 1926 St. Beuno's was the theologate of the English Province of the Society of Jesus. The word 'theologate' calls for comment. In the understanding of most people in Britain, a layman who aspires to the ministry, enrols at a theological college, follows a course there and at the end of his course is ordained. When used by Jesuits the word 'theologate' has a more specialised meaning. In chaff it is sometimes said that a Jesuit is ordained as a reward for a well-spent life, a remark which has just enough substance in it to cause a not-so-young Jesuit student to chafe. During the second half of the nineteenth century and for the first half of the twentieth, a youth coming to the English Province of the Society straight from school, normally faced the following obstacle course. For two years he would be a novice preparing to take his vows as a member of the Society. The vows duly taken, he would be termed a 'scholastic' until ordination made him a priest. His scholasticate began with two years of profane studies, during which he was a 'junior', or more grandly according to the official Latin 'Auditor Rhetoricae', a Student of Rhetoric. After that he became a 'philosopher' for three years. Then he would be sent to one of our schools to teach, a term which included not only classroom teaching, but games and disciplinary supervision of all kinds, especially in a boarding school, and whatever other chores were loaded onto him. In short, he was a general dogsbody in both school and community. Always undertrained and frequently overworked, he was often worth his weight in gold because of his energy and dedication, and sometimes through quite inculpable inaptitude, a liability to his colleagues and a source of exasperation to his headmaster. Many of my contemporaries spent five and six years under this arduous, unrespected but often quite enjoyable form of servitude. Only at the next stage did one become a 'theologian', actually studying theology in immediate preparation for ordination which took place after three years. Some of the newly ordained, and after 1913 all of them, stayed for a fourth

year. Even this was not the end. This came with the year of
tertianship, which really was the end of the beginning!

I have passed over the noviceship, the juniorate and the tertianship without elaboration because we shall meet these institutions
again as they come to rest temporarily at St. Beuno's. I have said
a little more about the period spent teaching because it immediately preceded the years of theology and had, I am sure, an
influence on them. For one thing, especially if the teaching lasted
several years, it meant that a man was about thirty years of age
when he began the course. It was rather old to be a student back
on the benches, listening to lectures, studying texts, being a mere
pupil among other pupils and facing another steeplechase of
examinations. Sober, devout, in many ways austere, it was not in
the full sense of the word an adult form of life. Moreover it was
being lived by men who had recently tasted something different.
The world of school is circumscribed, but it has its excitements, its
humour, its pathos, even its tragedies, and life with boys can never
be wholly predictable. This the theologian had now exchanged
for a life he had already experienced as a philosopher: hour-
long lectures in Latin, manuals and textbooks in that language
at its most pedestrian, and an order of the day, the week,
the year predictable in almost every detail. I have no doubt
that the average theologian studied conscientiously, relished the
gentlemanly cameraderie of the community and enjoyed what
diversions offered. I would also suspect that they did so in a spirit
of cheerful resignation, tinged with a certain weariness at their
long incubation, their eyes inwardly focussed on the prospect of
their approaching ordination and the man's work that lay beyond
it.

Not everyone was put through the entire drawn-out process I
have described. Older men omitted the juniorate, might only
spend two years in philosophy, then teach for only one year or
not at all. Consequently, the first year intake into theology might
include men whose years in the Society numbered only five,
alongside others who, having entered the noviceship straight from
school, had already notched up a good dozen. It always added
interest to one's first year in theology, that one was joined, not
only by one's fellow novices of one's own age, who had been
teaching, but by older men who had joined later, but had caught
one up. The mixture can be seen in the first year students of 1849,

listed in a letter of Charles Henry Collyns, who was a year ahead of them. Let us look at them individually.

Albany Christie, born in 1817 had been a fellow of Oriel College, Oxford, and had left to study medicine. He had come to the noviceship as late as 1847 and had therefore only completed two years in the Society, which is well beneath my five years minimum. I presume his Oxford studies exempted him from philosophy. Walter Clifford, a Stonyhurst boy, was born in 1820, and entered the Society in 1837, twelve years before beginning theology. Ralph Cooper, also of Stonyhurst, was born in 1821, became a novice in 1840 and came to St. Beuno's nine years later. Peter Gallwey, born in 1820, had left Stonyhurst for the noviceship in 1836, two months before his sixteenth birthday. With thirteen years in religious life he was technically the senior member of his year in 1849. Ignatius Grant, the son of a clergyman, was born in 1820, went to Oxford, but left without graduating, and entered the Society in 1842, seven years before arriving at St. Beuno's. Adam Laing Meason, who was born in Scotland in 1821 and educated at Stonyhurst, leaving there in 1840, had spent nine years in the Society. Edward Hood, the most venerable of the group, was born back in 1808. He was also a clergyman's son. He had been a conveyancer and was a devout member of a Ritualist congregation before becoming a Catholic and joining the noviceship in 1846. He therefore came to theology after three years, having one more year to his credit than Albany Christie. Richard Vaughan had been born only in 1826. He was obviously a precocious boy, entering Stonyhurst at nine and spending some time as a 'lay philosopher' before joining the noviceship in 1842 when he was not quite sixteen. I am still puzzled as to why he should have been sent to theology when not yet twenty-three. Superiors seem to have had second thoughts in the matter, because he was snatched away from St. Beuno's in midcourse to teach at Mount St. Mary's, and finished up being ordained two years after his former classmates. He was still only twenty-eight. Besides these eight members of the English Province there was a German scholastic named Muller and a diocesan student, William Clifford. Clifford was at St. Beuno's because Rome which had expelled both the Pope and the Jesuit General, and put so many theology professors to flight, had ceased for the time being to offer a suitable ambiance for seminary studies. He later became Bishop of Clifton.

Five Stonyhurst boys and three converts! The list shows how inbred the Province would have been without the influx of converts who came to it in the wake of the Oxford Movement, and what a major step Fr. Lythgoe had taken in starting two new schools. The group differs from most of its successors in that it would become harder to abbreviate philosophy, and almost impossible to avoid it, as had Christie. Hence my figure of five years as a minimum period before theology. The Stonyhurst monopoly would be gradually eroded and the proportion, though not the actual number, of converts tend to fall. Having met what would be known in America as 'the class of 1849', it is now worth our while to glance at their later careers.

Fr. Christie became Superior of St. Mary's Hall, in which philosophy was still studied but his chief work was done at Farm Street, London, where he spent thirty years. He was an eminent confessor and instructor of converts, and respected for his writings. A somewhat different achievement was his launching of an association of 'young work-girls' for whom he organised expeditions, even taking them as far afield as Paray-le-Monial. It is pleasant to think of this former member of the Oriel Senior Common Room chugging through France in the company of devout Eliza Doolittles. One hopes he let them see something of Paris. He died in 1891. Walter Clifford spent thirty-three years in the 'missions' of the Province. 'Missions' here does not refer to missionary work overseas, but to pastoral work in such places as Brough Hall and Pontefract. He lived till 1892. Ralph Cooper, poor man, spent much of his life as an invalid and often appears in the lists with the ominous words 'cur. val', which one might translate in the case of a younger man as 'on the sick list', and in the case of the old as 'now infirm'. Nevertheless he survived till 1894. Peter Gallwey made the big time. He became Prefect of Studies at Stonyhurst, Rector of Farm Street and then Master of Novices with Gerard Manley Hopkins under his wing for a year. He was appointed Provincial in 1873 and then Superior at St. Beuno's. He returned to Farm Street in 1877 and worked there till his death in 1906. He gave himself with distinction to 'preaching, instructing, confessing, giving retreats and missions, writing, assisting and supervising the publication of books and promoting every Catholic interest that came to his notice'. Adam Laing Meason, who had not only shown promise as a mathematician but helped with the teaching of theology, died in the summer of 1854 at the age of thirty-three. Fr. Grant piled up forty years of almost continuous 'mission' work in places like Liverpool, Edinburgh and Bristol, varied by two years as the English confessor in Paris and a year, presumably in the same capacity, in Boulogne. The English residents and visitors of those two cities must have offered something of a contrast to the slum children and convicts over whom he always took special pains. He was an invalid for at least the last eleven years of his life, dying at the age of eighty-four at St. Beuno's. Fr. Hood spent many years working at Wardour, Wiltshire and died there in 1886. Richard Vaughan, who as a scholastic had helped to make sense of St. Beuno's chapel, continued to exercise his practical talents, being Minister (Bursar) at Mount St. Mary's, Stonyhurst and Beaumont near Windsor. At the age of fifty he attended a course of chemistry lectures and then taught the subject at Liverpool until the age of sixty-six. He died in 1899 leaving extended and improved buildings in almost every place in which he had been employed.

This sample would be somewhat typical of the period 1848-1926 as a whole. One is struck by the fact that none of them went to America, Africa or Asia and that they saw so little of the colleges. In 1853 the year when most of them were ordained, the schools at Spinkhill and Liverpool were still small affairs, six men worked in Jamaica and one in Madura, and there were forty-eight 'missions' in England and Wales. As there were at that point only 101 priests in the Province, those missions claimed the majority of them. The picture would change. A school was started in Glasgow in 1859, Beaumont College near Windsor, another boarding school in 1861 and Preston Catholic College in 1865. There was further expansion towards the end of the century with Wimbledon in 1892, Stamford Hill, London, in 1894 and Leeds in 1905. Also the investment in the missions overseas would rise notably. Fifty years after the opening of St. Beuno's there would be thirty-three members of the Province at work in Jamaica, Honduras and Guiana and three priests on the Zambesi mission. From 7% in 1853 the proportion of priests of the English Province in the 'foreign missions' had in 1888 risen to 14%, in 1898 to 15%. Whereas the men of '49 spent their priestly lives in the 'home missions', their successors were more likely to be employed in the schools or overseas than in what came to be referred to as 'the parishes'.

There is another interesting and quite literally vital, anomaly about Albany Christie and his group. In 1867 a statistically minded Jesuit presented a study of the expectation of life of the members of the Society. He calculated that priests and scholastics dying between the years 1844 and 1865 had passed on average twenty-three years in the Society, the average age at death being forty-four. In 1900 another Jesuit with the same hobby states that those who died in 1899, including the brothers, had on average passed forty-one years in the Society, and reached the average age of sixty-four years and six months. Of our 1849 group two lived into their eighties, four into their seventies, only Laing Meason dying young. What interests me more than the uncharacteristic longevity of Christie and Co., and my curiosity will have to go unalloyed, is the effect, if any, on the outlook of a St. Beuno's student in the fifties and early sixties. They would know of every death in the Province. Unless the death was sudden, they would have been alerted to pray for the man when he was anointed, and later required by rule to pray for his soul. The dead man and the manner of his death would undoubtedly have been a topic of conversation when the news arrived. I should be surprised if they started adding up figures and calculating averages and drawing up conclusions about their own life expectancy. Yet the fact that English Jesuits averaged forty-four at the time of death when the ordinary Englishman of the period, once he had reached the age of twenty-one, could reasonably expect to live till sixty-two, must have impinged on their consciousness in at least some vague way. With what effect? Did it give them a sense of urgency, and contribute to an impatience to be ordained and at work? Did uncertainty of tenure bring an extra touch of piquancy to life? When they learned of the deaths within three months of one another in 1861 of the eighty-one year old George Oliver and the twenty-year old Walter Dickinson were they fatalistically resigned to the sheer randomness of the sour scythe and the blear share?

The reader is, no doubt, more interested to learn how the theologians lived than to enter into their attitude to death. For me there is no difficulty imagining their lives, but a great deal of difficulty in describing the same to other people. Substantially, their lives as theologians hardly differed from my own as a scholastic. It was a world in which I am no longer at home, but with which I am wholly familiar. In trying to depict it, therefore, I am liable to take too many things for granted. A second difficulty is with the sources. The obvious source is the Beadle's log. The Beadle, himself a student, was a combination of adjutant, Head Boy and shop steward. He was the liaison between the Rector and the students. He kept their lives moving along the grooves of tradition and promulgated whatever applications of traditional principles had been decided upon above. He kept a meticulous record of events to guide his successors, and from the recordings of his predecessors he offered guidance to his superiors and instructions to his peers. The importance of the log is of itself a guide to the mind of the time. Tradition was of immense and quite unquestioned moment. The present was substantially like the past with some accidental changes. The future should be kept like the past with whatever superficial modifications might be necessary carefully held to a minimum.

In 1926 the theologate moved to Heythrop in Oxfordshire and St. Beuno's became a tertianship. The Theologian's Log moved with them like the Ark of the Covenant. It was unthinkable that it should not. In 1952 I had greatness thrust upon me and, becoming Beadle, moved into the room where the shelved volumes of the Log—a century of them!—stood forever on parade, ready to guide me in all my decisions. Not knowing in 1952 the task that waited for me in 1989, I took little interest in the records of the St. Beuno's period, but did go page by page through the years when Hopkins was a theologian. There was little to show for my pains. I even found a piece of paper on which the few jejune entries concerning him had been listed by a previous researcher. The Beadles of 1874-7 did not know that their community contained a man whose importance in English literature would ensure that a century later the name of St. Beuno's would be heard, or at least read in print, wherever English literature is seriously studied. The limitation of the Log, of course, is that it is a mere record of events. It was not the Beadle's business to record his reflections, his hopes or fears nor those of his comrades.

One meets the same difficulty in three quite important articles about St. Beuno's, composed by Jesuits for Jesuits. The first, a double article of 1889 by John Pollen, was composed when the author was a student at St. Beuno's and was written for the entertainment of his contemporaries. So was the second, which was the work of Thomas Roberts in 1923. The third, produced for the centenary in 1948, was put together by Henry Keane. These were all men of stature; Fr. Pollen was to become a historian of repute; Thomas Roberts would be made Archbishop of Bombay, and was for my money the most inspiring member of the English Province in the twentieth century; Fr. Keane, writing in his old age, had held a series of important positions including those of Rector of St. Beuno's, Rector of Heythrop and Provincial. Their articles are readable, vivid, clearly authentic and are for the most part quite superficial. They do justice to the apostolic spirit of the house, listing the mass centres established by and served from St. Beuno's, describing the efforts to preach in Welsh, the catechising and the lectures given. For the rest they speak of the building, the problems of heating and of the water supply, the celebrations, the recreations, the highly inconvenient mischiming of the clock and the size of the honey yield. Nothing is said about the attitude of the theologians to the historical events on the continent which I have already mentioned, or to the major political and social issues of contemporary Britain, of their views on developments and controversies in the Church or their reactions to the books, ideas and philosophies which the period saw come to birth. No mention here of universal suffrage, of the Irish Question, of Darwin or von Hugel, of Browning or Swinburne and certainly not of Nietzsche, Baudelaire or Ibsen.

There are several reasons for this. In the first place the three writers are using the Beadle's Log, which, as I have made clear, merely records events. Secondly, as Jesuits writing for Jesuits there was much that they could leave unsaid. They did not have, for example, to comment on the inspiration which lay behind the lives of the St. Beuno's students, the Ignatian vision, the heroic tradition of the centuries of persecution and of survival throughout the period of the Suppression. They did not need to comment on the work for which the students were preparing themselves. I think that there is a third reason which I advance with trepidation. What I term to myself the Old English Province, the Province as it was in the second half of the nineteenth century and the first half of the twentieth, was for the most part an unspeculating and unreflecting Province. This was partly its Englishness. The English manage without a written constitution and are for the most part uncomfortable with ideologies. The English produce poets and respect scholars, but their admiration goes to the man who can manage things, and still more to the man who can manage men. This was particularly true of the Victorians. The workshop of the world had to be kept running and expanding. The distended cities and towns had to be administered and their growing populations protected from epidemics and delivered from their illiteracy. Then there was the White Man's Burden to be conscientiously shouldered throughout the greatest Empire the world had ever known. The English Jesuits were a part of this scene. In Britain they had to build new churches, put up elementary schools and develop their colleges. In Guyana and Southern Africa they became everything from architects to agriculturalists. They needed all the universal dexterity and inexhaustible resource of the pioneer, while wondering how to communicate gospel truths to Amerindians and Matabele. In consequence the Province evolved a collection of mechanisms in its schools, parishes and retreat houses, which its members served humbly, laboriously and certainly fruitfully. There was little of what we would call evaluation.

There were other reasons why the English Jesuits, while educated and in some respects cultivated, were not usually intellectual. A community like that of the theologians was, in spite of the contrasting backgrounds of some of the members, too homogeneous. They were all devout, orthodox Catholics preparing to spend the rest of their lives defending and propagating that faith. Such unanimity of belief and purpose does not promote the clash of minds at any depth. Also the Jesuit in formation was insulated from the outside world. Visits to or from 'externs', a term which covered anything human outside the Society of Jesus, were strictly controlled. Periodicals and reading matter in general had to present no danger to faith or morals. To consult a theological work by anyone other than a Catholic author required special permission. The young Jesuit's beliefs, objectives and priorities never received any authentic challenge, except perhaps in correspondence with an unbelieving relation or friend.

Even within the house itself a community like that of the theologians was a sealed group. The officials and lecturers formed one community, the theologians another and the laybrothers a third. On the whole they lived in different areas of the house, used different recreation rooms and had a somewhat different way of life. While wearing the same dress, with a slight variation for the brothers, and eating the same food, the three groups rarely came together. A scholastic who wandered into the kitchen or workshop and engaged the brothers in long conversations would soon find himself carpeted. Within the theologian's own community conversation was limited to the recognised periods and places. At other times silence was to be observed, and it was a disciplinary offence to go to someone else's room except over some practical matter which could be quickly despatched. Even that was supposed to be done in Latin. So, no sitting in someone else's room tiring the sun with talking and sending him down the sky as one put the world to rights. No hearing the chimes at midnight as the debate wandered over all the things that are, and all the things that might be.

This is not to say that the theologians never talked to one another heart to heart. They could have done so on walks, as we often did. I should be surprised if a number of them did not ignore the 'rule of rooms' as often as I was to do in another place and at another time, but also as a theologian under the same set of regulations. Nor am I saying that the Province never produced men of an independent and vigorous cast of mind. It patently did, but did so in spite of its much cherished Anglo-Saxon practicality, and against the deadening effect of a long training which kept its students cocooned together, unstimulated by contact with anyone who believed or lived differently, unstirred by books or periodicals which might challenge their beliefs or way of life, and discouraged in practice, from any authentic exploration by discussion even among themselves.

VI

The day within and time out

Fr. Collyns' letter of 1850, which I have quoted before, sets out the order of the day which he and his contemporaries followed:

5.00-a.m.   Rise
            Spiritual Duties till 7.00
7.00-7.45   Study
8.00   Breakfast
        Study
10.00-12.30   Classes in dogmatic or moral theology or canon law or ecclesiastical history
1.00   Dinner
2.30-3.00   Hebrew for the First Year
3.30   Evening Dogma
4.30   Recreation till 5.00
        Study till 6.40
10.00-p.m.   Bed

There are gaps in that horarium which the recipient of the letter could fill in for himself and technical terms which he would have readily understood. I had better fill in the former and explain the latter. Spiritual duties in the early morning would consist of an hour's meditation and Mass. Before dinner everyone would spend a quarter of an hour in 'Examination of Conscience'. After dinner there would be a period of recreation which would be spent walking in the garden in groups of three unless rain forced them into the recreation room. 'Evening dogma' means that there was an evening class in Dogmatic Theology. One 'professor' would lecture on one part of the course in the morning and his colleague on a quite different part in the evening. Scripture, which was certainly studied, seems to have got left off the list. Fr. Collyns brings his day to an end rather abruptly. He has omitted supper, evening recreation, which in winter time would be in the recreation room with a large log fire, and the evening spiritual duties, perhaps Litanies of the Saints or Benediction of the Blessed Sacrament followed by the preparation of the next day's meditation and a further examination of conscience. At least twice a week there was a 'circle' or formal disputation, which I shall describe later. In Fr. Collyns' day they took place in the evening, probably at 5.00-p.m. On Monday evening there was a 'case' of moral theology to be discussed.

A century later, when I was a first year theologian, the day's programme had evolved in two ways. The day started later, and we had much less study time available. Our rising bell rang at 6.00-a.m. As we went to bed at 10.30-p.m., we had a half hour more of sleep. We had less study time because we did not have that ghastly sounding three quarters of an hour study before breakfast, and we spent more time at lectures. The morning was taken up by three hour-long lectures, and in the evening we also had 'evening dogma', often followed by a fifth lecture on some additional subject such as Liturgical History or the Oriental Churches. The passage of a century had not wrought any sweeping changes in the life of the Jesuit student of Theology. Certainly not in the English Province. Both in Fr. Collyns' day and my own the scholastic was also privately responsible for such daily obligations as the recitation of the rosary, an evening visit to the Blessed Sacrament and a quarter of an hour's 'spiritual reading' i.e. of some book which would contribute to his appreciation and practice of things spiritual, not merely further his intellectual grasp of them.

It was a rhythmical life of prayer and study in an atmosphere of silence and clerical decorum lived in a somewhat monastic building deep in the countryside, but the inmates remained sons of St. Ignatius. Their predecessors had risked, and sometimes forfeited, their lives to maintain and spread the True Faith. They themselves were Jesuits for the same purpose. The house existed to train apostles, so how could they ignore the harvest field of North Wales when they lived in the middle of it, and when there was no Catholic mission south of Talacre and Holywell other than Bangor? The staff, the fourth year students who were already ordained, and the scholastics seized whatever possibility of apostolic work offered itself.

In 1851, Fr. James Etheridge, who had lately succeeded his brother John as Rector, began to say Mass on Sundays 'in one of the parlours of a public house kept by a Catholic; the congregation consisting of the landlord, his wife and the families of three

Irishmen employed upon the railroad'. James was later to be a Bishop in British Guiana and Apostolic Delegate in Haiti. I wonder if in the middle of some crowded episcopal ceremony in Demerara his mind ever wandered back to those four families gathered round him in a pub in Rhyl. From that public house the growing congregation moved to the disused Assembly Rooms, which they rented for a church and school. Then some land was purchased and a church capable of holding 150 people was erected upon it. Soon this building too was outgrown by the expanding congregation of residents and summer visitors and a much larger church was built and opened in 1862 out of the patrimony of Fr. John Griffiths-Wynne. Fr. Wynne, as he was commonly known, was an old Etonian who had been elected a Fellow of All Souls in 1841, and had visited Pope Pius IX in exile at Gaeta while he was still an Anglican. Received into the Catholic Church during Easter Week in 1850 in Jerusalem, he studied and was ordained at the Academia Ecclesiastica in Rome. After completing his D.D. studies he entered the noviceship in 1857. He was not only a scholar, but had been a notable athlete in his youth and remained 'an excellent shot as well as a skilful fisherman'. He had travelled a good deal in Italy, sometimes in the company of Edward Lear, and also in the Near East. The Catholics of Rhyl had the services of this habitue of Oxford, Rome and Jerusalem from 1860 to 1866.

In 1852 a chapel was opened in St. Asaph where in the words of Fr. Wynne, 'under the very shadow of the Protestant cathedral a quadrangular collection of huts had long become the permanent camping ground of some of the emigrants from the Sister Isle'. I cannot resist quoting his description of the situation in 1862, 'a colony of poor Irish under the social incubus of the Protestant Bishop, Dean and Chapter . . . and the sleepy, wealthy, comfortable yet lifeless atmosphere which pervades the cathedral towns of Protestant England'. Did this learned gentleman of undoubted Welsh descent and Welsh connections forget that St. Asaph is not in England? How little his learning and travel had done to mitigate the odium theologicum of the period! And how surprised he would have been to learn that in 1987 the Bishop of St. Asaph and all his Welsh episcopal colleagues would come in a body to St. Beuno's to have lunch, to meet the staff, and discuss in what way the resources of St. Beuno's might meet the needs of their own clergy and people!

The few Catholics in Denbigh were provided with Sunday Mass if they cared to travel the three miles to Llewesog Hall, the residence of the Ainsworth family. In 1856 a room was hired in Denbigh itself, and a church opened there six years later in 1862. Two years after that a chapel was established in Ruthin, which, being about twelve miles away, was the most far flung of the St. Beuno's missions. In all these ventures the provision of a school came a close second to the arranging of a Sunday Mass. The hired Assembly Rooms in Rhyl doubled for a time as a mass centre and a school. A part of the building erected in Denbigh provided 'a cottage for the schoolmistress'. The Beadle's log mentions a scholastic being sent to Liverpool 'to find a schoolmistress for St. Asaph'. The schoolchildren were the unpriested scholastics' chance. The scholastics catechised them devotedly at St. Beuno's itself, in Rhuddlan and of course at St. Asaph, Denbigh and Ruthin. They also gave lantern shows and lectures; the latter, of course, not to children. In those self-improving, cinemaless days, lectures, with or without slides, could be quite a draw.

Fr. Wynne describes a course of three lectures delivered by one of the Theologians, 'We were at that time building a church and forming a congregation at Rhyl, and Rhyl became a centre of furious attacks from the Protestant Alliance and all the fanatics of the neighbourhood. Scurrilous pamphlets and articles in the local newspapers appeared in which the old bugbear of the 'blind obedience of the Jesuits' was much insisted on. Father Law, although he was only a student, not yet a priest, came down to Rhyl, and gave three lectures in my school which were well attended by both Catholics and Protestants, on 'The blind obedience of the Jesuits compared with the discipline in Her Majesty's Navy'. The lecturer, Augustus Law, had held the rank of Second Lieutenant in the Navy. After ordination he was to work in Demerara for five years, return for his tertianship, spend three years in Scotland and then be sent out to South Africa. There he would die at the age of forty-seven from exhaustion, under-nourishment, dysentery and yellow fever on a pioneering visit to the kraal of King Umzila of the Abagasi.

Symptomatic of the impulsive yet persevering zeal of those early days are the determined efforts which some of them made to learn Welsh, while fully aware that they were in Wales only for three or four years, and that their future work lay outside the Principality.

Soon after his arrival at St. Beuno's Albany Christie, whom we have already met, the former Fellow of Oriel, approached the Rector as the spokesman of a group who proposed to study Welsh in order to preach in it. The Rector acquiesced suppressing, one suspects, his reservations. Ignatius Grant, a canny Scot in spite of his English education, was quite explicit. 'Let us pray and strive for the conversion of a Welsh-speaking Parson or Scholar. A native priest will do more by himself, knowing the people, than all of us put together'. Christie and Co. worked hard and had the confidence to deliver an address regularly after Sunday Benediction. This they, and their sucessors after them, continued to do, until it became all too evident even to the most ardent, that their performances were little understood and appreciated even less.

Gerard Manley Hopkins, forever fascinated by words, was attracted to Welsh from the beginning. Having arrived at St. Beuno's on 28th August 1874, on the 29th he is saying to his father, 'I have half a mind to get up a little Welsh', and three days later writes, 'I am trying a little Welsh. It is complicated but euphonious and regular'. Then comes one of his Hamlet-ish tussels of conscience: 'Indeed in coming here I began to feel a desire to do something for the conversion of Wales. I began to learn Welsh too but not with a very pure intention perhaps'. After some vacillation, unlike the Prince, he came to a positive decision and seems to have had lessons from a Miss Susannah Jones, and was allowed to stay with her brother Fr. John Jones at Caernarvon, the only Catholic priest in Wales capable of preaching in Welsh. In January '77 he can say, 'I have learnt Welsh, as you say; I can read easy prose and can speak stumblingly, but at present I find the greatest difficulty, amounting mostly to total failure, is understanding it when spoken and the poetry, which is quite as hard as the choruses in a Greek play—and consider what those would be with none but a small and bad dictionary at command—I can make little way with'. The man who had graduated with First Class Honours had presumably overcome the difficulty of translating Greek choruses, and he made sufficient way with Welsh poetry to try his hand at it himself, and to be much influenced by it. He would later write of 'my Welsh days . . . my salad days, when I was fascinated with cynghanedd or consonant-chime' and readily admitted the influence of his Welsh reading on his English poetry. 'The chiming of consonants I got in part from the Welsh'. That

Gerard was permitted his lessons and his stay at Caernarvon suggests that superiors were still respectful to a spontaneous interest in Welsh, or that they were somewhat indulgent towards Gerard himself. Perhaps both.

During my own novitiate in this house and during my tertian-ship of 1955-56, I could not see the slightest interest in the Welsh language, nor any sign of anyone having recently entertained such an interest. This was understandable. Since 1926 St. Beuno's had been the Tertianship house; the Tertians were here only for nine months, and while here lived a straitly enclosed life with a minimum of outside contacts. When I came back in 1985, the first thing I noticed on the way from the station was that the road signs had become bi-lingual. A few days later I learned that the local children can now receive their entire education through the medium of the Welsh tongue. None of the Jesuits working here today can speak Welsh, which most of us see as a lack, and about which we are rather apologetic. Our retreatants come from all over Britain and the English speaking world, and sometimes from places outside it, so that Welsh is not of itself relevant to the work of the house. We still feel our ignorance to be an impoverishment, an estrangement from our context. Our Superior, to his credit, has taught himself the Lord's Prayer in Welsh, listens to appropriate records and tapes, honours Ann Griffiths and supports the Welsh XV. He renders our Welsh scenery in charming water colours, but I do not expect him to try his hand at cynghanedd.

In spite of its discouraging results the Welsh Class died hard. It was certainly in existence in 1865 'to help us to be of some service to the poor people around us who are unable to speak English'. The quotation is taken from a list of extra-curricular activities given in a report for that year. It also mentions an English Academy which 'exhibited a weekly essay in English on some subject connected with Sacred Learning, and what the writer calls 'lighter studies' namely 'Architecture, Antiquities, Botany, the minute animal life of Infusoria'. Here we have the typical interests of a cultivated Victorian gentleman. At some time the Essay Society seems to have replaced the English Academy, its range of subjects being wider and less austere in tone. Two of the early accounts of past days at St. Beuno's, to which I have referred, were written for the Essay Society. The entertainments and relaxa-tions of the Theologians are those of their period and class. The entertainments were largely homemade; there were plays and concerts provided by themselves, with a few guests invited on greater occasions. There were debates and spelling bees. Hopkins, as was appropriate in an outstanding wordsmith, won one of the latter.

Geology and archaeology seem to have been very popular, providing simultaneously intellectual interest, fresh air and sometimes strenuous exercise. Ironically, the first generations of St. Beuno's diggers, while trying to reconstruct the past, left no record of their own doings. It was only towards the end of the century that their activities were formally set down. In 1895 George Pollen came to theology. He had once studied petrology in the Royal School of Mines and subsequently worked as an applied chemist in Russia. He and his assistants explored the caves opposite Ffynnon Beuno, turning up many flint artifacts. More dramatic, or more melodramatic, were their doings on the far side of the valley at Ty Newydd. They rented a cottage for a year in order to have legal access to the site, and then gained physical access by removing 'a hundred tons of rock with blasting powder and dynamite'. That must have made a pleasant change from Latin lectures on the Hypostatic Union or Trinitarian Circuminsession! Fr. Pollen's successors, John Luck and Philip Stapleton, led the excavation of five tumuli at Bryngwyn Hall. In 1908 Kenelm Digby-Beste, a man of legendary energy, arrived. 'To his initiative and perseverance Disserth (sic) owes the disclosing of Siamber Wen, a thirteenth century dwelling which was buried in undergrowth, and now stands a ruin for the inspection of tourists'. The work done on these occasions was of sufficiently high standard for its results to be recorded in such periodicals as The Quarterly Journal of the Geological Society, British Association Reports and Archaeologia Cambrensis. After his ordination and tertianship George Pollen was sent to take charge of the studies at St. Stanislaus College in British Guiana, but returned after nine years. He finally died at Preston aged sixty-seven. Fr. Stapleton taught in South Africa and Rhodesia, doing further archaeological work during the holidays and dying at sixty-four. Fr. Digby-Beste went to Bulawayo where he died at thirty-nine. Fr. Luck served more prosaically in such places as Lancashire, Bristol and Farm Street, living till the age of eighty-five.

Other forms of exercise had less cultural motivation. A favourite sport, particularly in the 'fifties', was the otterhunt. As participation in this form of venery was by invitation only, St. Beuno's students were evidently accepted by the local gentry as social equals and congenial companions. The suspicion of 'Papists' and Jesuits had obviously been disarmed at least in that social stratum. To us the hunting to death of such a graceful and interesting animal as the otter is quite repugnant. The mid-Victorians had no such qualms, especially as the otter preys on fish, and fishing was another favourite activity of the Theologians. Most of these men had already spent three years at St. Mary's Hall, Stonyhurst, where they would have fished the River Hodder and generally grown accustomed to these country sports, into which many of them had already been initiated by their own families. At Stonyhurst they would also have tramped the Fells, and so developed the robust leg muscles which continued to serve them at St. Beuno's. The theologians were prodigious walkers, as they demonstrated conspicuously during the 'villa' holidays of which more hereafter. Team games emerge quite late in the story. The 'flanks of the voel' are hardly a place for a soccer pitch, still less for a cricket flat. Nor would it have been easy to find twenty-two enthusiasts in a community which in 1870 numbered thirty and in 1880 forty-four, with an average age of over thirty and by no means all of them Britons. However, in 1892, when the community was nudging fifty, permission was granted for football. The pitch, parts of which were almost flat, was laid out in a field halfway up the mountain, there to be visited by many a 'bright wind boisterous' which snatched our ball away down some 'air-built thoroughfare'. In 1898 Fr. Provincial stated that he had no objection to the community playing golf, and a course was ingeniously constructed, which, beginning above the terraces, reached even beyond our elevated football field.

Jesuit institutions on the continent were normally located in cities and towns and the larger of them usually acquired a property somewhere outside the town to which the community could sometimes escape to breathe a cleaner air and enjoy the countryside. The English Jesuit school at St. Omers had such a country refuge or 'Villa House' at Blandecques, simplified by the English into Blandyke. Two hundred years after the loss of St. Omers, English scholastics would celebrate one Thursday a month a little more elaborately than their other free days, and call that day 'a Blandyke'. The word 'Villa', similarly fossilized, was used for the annual fortnight's holiday. In 1853 'Villa' was at Barmouth. Everyone left the house at 3.00-a.m. to walk to Denbigh, where they took an omnibus to Pentrefoelas, and there took to their feet again for the next fourteen miles or so to Ffestiniog. Four men actually walked the whole distance, something of the order of forty miles, and very few of them on the flat. It rained the whole day. They gave themselves a day in Ffestiniog to rest and dry out, and on the following day they walked ten miles to Portmadog for breakfast, which left a mere sixteen or so to Barmouth. Even greater feats were performed on the return journey via Corwen and Llangollen. Accounts of the various adventures and misadventures experienced when 'messing about in boats' are to be found in Thomas Roberts' account of the period.

Sometimes the strenuous recreational activities of the Theologians left their own memorial, the outstanding example being the Rock Chapel. It was on Boxing Day, 1862, that the Rector, Fr. Lambert 'made an appeal to the community for a corps of volunteers, sappers and miners, or rather navvies and engineers, to undertake the public works at the Rock, which during the present year had become College property. It was manifestly the duty of Ours to see that the charms of the Rock be no longer inaccessible'. 'Ours' was a term commonly employed to designate our fellow Jesuits, a single specimen being 'one of Ours', a term which, I think, other people found unpalatable at best. Whether it sprang from Christmas goodwill, a wish to work off Christmas fare or a genuine interest in the project, there was a ready response to the Rector's appeal. 'Sat. 27th. Volunteers at work both morning and evening . . . Mon. 29th. Volunteers at work . . . Luncheon at the Rock at noon'. Much of Christmas week went in the same way. There is no hint at this stage of any intention to build a chapel, and no record at all of who conceived it. It is in March 1866 that the foundation stone was laid. The building was complete before the end of September. According to the Bishop's letter of approval, written in the baroque style then considered appropriate for ecclesiastical communications, 'a chapel dedicated to the Virgin, Mother of God, mourning her only-begotten son has been built upon the rock known as St. Michael's, near the College of St. Beuno's . . . from whence a view can be obtained far and wide over a district once most devout to this same Mother, and which today is filled with the ruins of sacred shrines where the Christian people were wont to assemble . . . ' The Bishop's letter implies, and tradition declares that the chapel was intended as an act of reparation for the abandonment and decay of so many mediaeval Lady shrines in the area.

The chapel was inaugurated on September 24th 1866, when its architect, Ignatius Scoles, offered his first mass there. The chapel had not been designed by an amateur. Fr. Scholes was the son of a church architect and had himself been trained in that profession. Born in 1834 he joined the Society at the age of twenty-six and after ordination spent six years in Guiana. Returning to Europe for his tertianship, he spent six years in Preston and then returned to Guiana. There he planned churches and chapels and improved others; he became Vicar-General, spent three hours every evening among the poor of Georgetown, received innumerable converts, and died in his sixty-second year.

1862, when St. Beuno's acquired the Rock Chapel Field and its picturesque rock, was also the year in which it was presented with the head of a mediaeval cross, which is now set on a plinth in the front quadrangle. This is no commonplace mediaeval fragment. It is all that remains of the renowned Tremeirchion Rood of Grace, whose wonders were sung in the reign of Henry VII by the bard Gruffydd ap Ieuan ap Llewelyn Vychau. The broken crosshead was discovered lying under a yew-tree in Tremeirchion churchyard by a Mr. Hinde, a devout Catholic, who was later to fight as a volunteer to defend the Papal States. He bought the stone from the churchwardens for the not negligible sum of £5, and it was carried away in a cart to St. Beuno's. The crosshead was given its present setting in 1910 by Kenelm Digby-Beste whose vigorous—using that word both literally and metaphorically—interest in the mediaeval we have met before. 'To him St. Beuno's owes the transformation of its entrance from the roughness of a backyard to its present suitableness. He built the rockery, and laid out the setting for the ancient Tremeirchion Cross. His efforts obtained the indulgence from the Bishop and organised the blessing of the restored cross with the singing of the hymn that had been its own in the far-off Catholic days of the valley'.

VII

The Longs and the Shorts of it

Fr. Lythgoe had built St. Beuno's not to rear otterhunters, amateur archaeologists and marathon walkers or even to provide catechists for the families of Irish labourers. He wanted an annual crop of capable priests. It was to be 'my theologate' where aspiring pastors learned their trade. For this they required a general practical competence in preaching, hearing confessions, administering the sacraments and generally tending Christ's flock. At the same time an order whose origin lay in the University of Paris, which had produced theological writers of the first importance and which had been in the forefront of European education, had to aim at something more than the training of pastoral plumbers. This ambivalence of aim the Society had realistically tried to resolve by instituting two parallel courses, the rough equivalent of an Honours course and the Pass degree at a secular university. The 'Long Course' in theology lasted four years with ordination at the end of the third year. The 'Short Course' took three years with ordination normally, but not invariably, at the end of the second. From 1893 the men of both courses were ordained together at the end of three years, the 'Shorts' going off to their first posts, the 'Longs' staying on for their fourth year. From the ranks of the latter would come Provincials, lecturers in Philosophy and Theology and, with exceptions, Novicemasters and Instructors of Tertians. In the first part of this century the 'Shorts' men would sometimes refer to themselves as the 'cabhorses' of the Province. The term did not seem to have any correlative, so I shall never know whether they thought of their more academically equipped brethren as cavalry chargers, as racehorses or as drawing the conveyances of the aristocracy.

The official terminology of this bifurcation has its own interest. In the earliest lists we have 'Auditores Theologiae' i.e. Students (literally, 'hearers') of Theology, and 'Auditores Theologiae Moralis', Students of Moral Theology, as though the second group were to remain innocent of Dogmatic Theology. In 1873 the latter

term changes to 'Auditores Cursus Moralis et Theologiae Ab-
breviatae'. One wonders whether the teachers of Dogma had
fought and won some battle to get recognition of the fact that
the 'Shorts' men did have some need of their subject. In 1886
the longer course is labelled 'Auditores Theologiae Scholasticae',
which I think can reasonably translate as 'Students of Academic
Theology'. In 1913, when both courses became equally of four
years duration, they were sensibly called the 'Major' and 'Minor'
courses. The English Province, with its instinctive preference for
tradition over logic, continued to talk of 'Longs' and 'Shorts'.

Even the 'Longs' men, to their credit, thought of themselves as
future pastors, rather than as potential Doctors of Theology, and
this fact, together with the national predilection for the practical,
meant that the subject taken most seriously was Moral Theology.
Moral Theology was a brave, and perhaps at times presumptuous,
attempt to decide on the morality or immorality of every possible
action in which human free choice was involved. It dealt with
everything one might do in private or in public, as a single
individual or as a member of a family, as a member of a society,
as a member of a profession or of the Church. It covered deed,
word and all deliberate thought. A priest hearing confessions or
being consulted outside the confessional, was expected to be able
to declare whether any action committed or merely contemplated,
was legitimate or sinful, whether grieviously or venially so. Part of
the art was the ability to recognise the complex or very special
case which was outside one's competence, and the willingness to
ask for time to consult the accepted 'authors' or some acknowledged expert. This subject was carefully taught and rigorously
examined. No-one would be ordained unless he showed both an
adequate grasp of the theory and sufficient practical skill. The
course lasted two years. In addition to the lectures there was each
week a 'case', in which some hypothetical moral situation was
analysed and discussed. All four years attended the 'case' and
every priest in the house would come to at least one a month. As
I have already pointed out, the 'Short' course known for
many years as Auditores Theologiae Moralis', as though their
dogmatic studies were negligible, which indeed they may have
been.

Church History and Canon law were studied in the first two
years; Scripture in the third and fourth. A priest had to have some

knowledge of the working of ecclesiastical law. Without it he and his parishioners would soon have been in a fine muddle. Church History provided a background to dogma and was obviously required for any understanding of the Church. That Scripture should have run a poor third to Dogma and Moral Theology may seem scandalous. I think that the justification, unstated and perhaps often unrealised, was as follows. The Bible, that collection of works of quite different literary species, written at different periods and in a variety of contexts, requires interpretation. That is one of the functions of the Church. The laity are taught by the priests, the priests by the theologians and the theologians work under the jurisdiction of the ecclesiastical authorities. The dogmatic theologians taught us what to believe, the moral theologians what we might or might not do morally, and the ascetical theologians taught one the way to holiness. The Bible was greatly to be revered; it was a source of 'proof texts'; it, together with the experience of the Church, was the source of which the dogmatic, moral and ascetical theologians drew. Because they had done so diligently, their digests were of more practical utility than the inspired text taken, as it were, raw.

Dogmatic Theology, if we judge by the number of lectures and the solemnity of examinations, was theoretically the most important subject of all. Dogmatic Theology aims at expressing Christian beliefs in precise, coherent terms and combining them into a logical whole. At St. Beuno's, as at most seminaries, the concepts used and the philosophical principles invoked were drawn from what has been described by a sympathetic historian as 'an uninspired Scholastic Aristotelianism'. The terminology, of course, was not that of the original Greek, but the Latin rendering current in the Middle Ages. The dominant theologians of mediaeval Western Europe had used the Aristotelian metaphysic as they understood it, and their usages, commonly with further misinterpretation, were reapplied by the Catholic theologians of subsequent centuries. The drawback is obvious: a conceptual system worked out in the Middle Ages was hard put to it to assimilate the ideas and categories of later scholarship, of subsequent original philosophical investigation and especially the discoveries of empirical science. The use of Latin involved similar disadvantages. Latin was the official language of the Catholic Church, of its liturgy and administration and had been the lingua franca of the learned world as late as the publication of Newton's 'Naturalis Philosophiae Principia Mathematica'. Its disadvantage was that it had long ago ceased to be anyone's mother tongue and had therefore lost the flexibility and creativity of a living language.

Whereas there was a weekly 'case of conscience' as part of the course of Moral Theology, in Dogmatic Theology there were two 'disputations'. A 'defendant' had to give a short exposition of some doctrine, mention opposed opinions, summarise whatever 'proof' was to be found in Scripture, in the writings of the Fathers and in the authoritative decrees of Councils and Popes, and then refute the arguments of two 'objicients'. The objections had to be proferred in syllogisms. The whole process—provided one's Latin was up to it—was clear and logical, but at a considerable price. The doctrine under discussion had to be stated in a 'thesis', preferably a single sentence such as, 'Secundam Personam Sanctissimae Trinitatis esse Deum probatur ex Sacris Scripturis, ecclesiaeque universalis traditione', (that the Second Person of the Holy Trinity is Divine is shown by both Sacred Scripture and the universal tradition of the Church). The exposition had to be highly compact, the mention of dissentient opinions almost contemptuously cursory, while the proofs were reduced to little more than quotations from the relevant passages of Scripture, the Fathers and the statements of Councils. It was effective pedagogy, and yet educationally impoverishing. It focused on what were considered essentials, but did not allow for nuances, for the tentative, for those accumulations of indications and hints which are so important in scholarship. The 'objicient' or adversary had to reduce what were subtle and complex linguistic and historical arguments to the inappropriate and unaccommodating form of the syllogism, while the use of Latin confined him in practice to the terminology, concepts and categories of the traditional position. He had been invited to give battle, but with one hand tied behind his back and while standing on one leg.

As a result of this system of training, the average Jesuit absorbed a respect for logic and clarity, and could be relied on to express the faith with impeccable orthodoxy, but if taken outside the Neo-Scholastic metaphysic and traditional terminology, he became a fish out of water gasping for his familiar element. There was a significant difference between the training in Moral Theology and the instruction in Dogma. Moral Theology, with the exception of the single year, 1877-78, was always taught by a member of the English Province, and in the early decades by men of much practical and administrative experience. Although textbooks and the substance of the lectures were in Latin, care was taken to see that the student could not only deal with confessional matters in English, but that he was able to interpret the euphemisms and even argot of his likely penitents. The examination in the theory of Moral was conducted in Latin, but the exam for the hearing of confessions was in English. Dogma, in contrast, was for some time taught mainly by Jesuits from the continent; there was no exam requiring the student to express the doctrines of the Church in non-technical language, and no test for preaching which required the same capacity for interpretation demanded of the confessor.

Besides the weekly disputations there were performances, and I use that noun deliberately, normally twice a year, at which a selected champion offered to joust in defence, not of one thesis, but of several covering most of a term's work. He was not supposed to know beforehand which theses the two objicients would choose to dispute. When as a philosopher I had the role of defendant thrust upon me, a soft-hearted objicient could not stop himself dropping the broadest hints the evening before combat. The heroic performance, which could make a man a legend in his own time, was the 'Grand Act' in which the student offered to defend the whole of Dogmatic Theology. I can only find two such Herculean performances in the entire history of St. Beuno's. In 1862 Fr. James Harris defended 'Universa Theologia' ('All Theology') expressed in 102 theses. James, born in 1824, had had but a rudimentary education, after which he became a hosier's clerk in London. That he was no run-of-the-mill shop assistant he demonstrated by becoming, at the age of seventeen, a popular public speaker during the anti-Corn-Law agitation. Some years later he compassionately attempted to rescue an Irish lad, 'who attended upon him in his lodging', from his Popish superstitions and in the process convinced himself of the truth of the Catholic claims. He joined the Society in 1850, leaving a young lady 'overwhelmed with grief'. He studied philosophy at Namur while simultaneously teaching English in the Jesuit school. He proved so effective a teacher and disciplinarian that the Belgian Jesuits, asked and were granted, his services for another four years after

the completion of his philosophy studies. At the end of four
years 'Theology' he performed the 'Grand Act', 'which', says his
chronicler 'taking into account his deficiency in the classical languages, was on the whole satisfactory'. It sounds as though his
audience showed themselves less enthusiastic than the anti-Corn-
Law crowd which had applauded him 'with universal cheers and
waving of handkerchiefs'. After this theological tour-de-force Fr.
Harris stayed at St. Beuno's, teaching Church History for one year,
being Minister during a second and teaching Moral Theology
during a third. Then he was sent to St. Francis Xavier's College,
Liverpool where his over-exacting, but very effective, work undoubtedly shortened his life. He died in 1883.

The other 'Grand Act' was staged in 1904 with Fr. George
Hayward Joyce as the defendant and the material condensed this
time into eighty theses. George H. Joyce was no hoiser's clerk.
Born in 1864, the son of the Vicar of Harrow-on-the-Hill, he had
been to Charterhouse, had held a Classics Scholarship at Oriel and
studied at both Leipzig and Bonn. He had held two curacies
before becoming a Catholic and then a novice in 1893. After
his 'Grand Act' he went to St. Mary's Hall, Stonyhurst, where
he taught the scholastics Logic and General Metaphysics, and
wrote 'Principles of Logic', which went through three editions. In
1909 he was recalled to St. Beuno's to teach Dogma. When the
Theologians moved in 1926 to Heythrop, Oxfordshire, he went
with them, continuing to lecture until his death in 1943. Having
been transferred from Philosophy to Theology he wrote 'The
Catholic Doctrine of Grace', 'Principles of Natural Theology' and
'Christian Marriage'. Besides these solid, well received works he
wrote a large number of pamphlets and articles, some of the latter
being for the 'Catholic Encyclopaedia' and 'Hastings Encyclopaedia
of Religion and Ethics'. His was a life of substantial theological
achievement, adequately adumbrated by that scene in the Chapel
(Yes! It was held in the Chapel) in 1904, when this slight man,
normally very hesitant, expounded and argued from 10.00 a.m. to
12.40 p.m. and 3.30 to 5.00 p.m., taking on, two by two, no less
than eight objicients.

When Fr. Joyce joined the staff at St. Beuno's in 1909 his arrival
meant that both Dogma professors were, for the first time since
1863, both members of the English Province. As the partnership of
'62 to '63 had lasted only a single year, it is plain what difficulty

the English Province had in this area. When Fr. Lythgoe set up 'my theologate' he was taking a gamble—or should I say 'relying heavily on Providence'—that a team of lecturers could somehow be conjured into existence and then maintained. It was the second part of the operation which, as we shall see, caused the greater difficulties.

During the nineteenth century and into the twentieth the theologate was considered to be adequately staffed if six posts were filled. These were: two Dogma Professors, a Professor of Moral, of Scripture, of Church History and Canon Law taken together and someone to take charge of the 'Short' course. Everyone was called a 'professor'. Someone teaching boys in a school was a 'master'; if he were asked to teach Jesuits be became a 'professor'. Thus Hopkins, when teaching the Jesuits immediately after their noviceship, was a 'Professor of Rhetoric'. The word means a good deal less than is implied in British academic circles by the occupancy of a 'Chair'. The first team of professors fielded at St. Beuno's consisted of the Rector, John Etheridge, who taught Moral, of two Swiss refugees, Ketterer and Sautier, and two more from Rome, Perrone and Mazio. It was plainly a brittle arrangement, and within two years both pairs had been recalled. Dogma was then taught for two years by Frs. Forn (Aragon) and Cardella (Rome) with a Fr. Agus from Turin looking after Scripture. 'Shorts' seem to have been taught by a different person every year, a pattern which was to recur frequently before the end of the century. Quite often no-one is specifically assigned to them, the gap presumably being filled by a teacher of some other subject resignedly 'doubling up'. What with the brevity of their course and the totally makeshift fashion of their teaching, it is a wonder that the 'Shorts' learned any dogma at all!

In 1851 John Etheridge left to assume the office of Provincial, his elder brother James replacing him, not only as Rector, but also as Professor of Moral Theology. For the Rector to discharge both offices was for some years almost a matter of course, the appointment being made, one suspects, in the light of the man's capacity for government, rather than on the grounds of his qualifications as a Professor of Moral. In 1852 Fr. Forn was replaced by an Irishman, Fr. Edmund O'Reilly, who had taught for twelve years at the Irish seminary of Maynooth before becoming a Jesuit. Fr. Raffo (Turin) took over the baton of Scripture from Fr. Agus, and

'Shorts' were taught for a year by Fr. Meason, who had but two years to live. Fr. Raffo left after two years; Fr. O'Reilly, who was to join Newman at the new Catholic University in Dublin, after three. The team was once more reconstituted in 1855 when James Etheridge left for Preston and was succeeded by William Card-well with the title of Vice-Rector, and two more Irishmen, Fr. W. Kelly and Fr. D. Jones, arrived to plug gaps and keep the English scholastics advancing to ordination. When the Irish Province decided to emulate the English, and set up their own theologate, Frs. Kelly and Jones were naturally required to rally to the venture, their withdrawal bringing to the ground the whole flimsy structure yet again.

Fr. Lythgoe's two year old corpse may have turned in its East Anglian grave when in September '57 the decision was announced that all members of the 'Long Course' would be sent abroad for theology. This was not an unreasonable step. The Province at that point contained about 115 priests. It still had numerous missions in England, three colleges and commitments overseas. There were novices, juniors and philosophers to be provided for, and not every member of the Province was hale and hearty and ready for anything. To concentrate temporarily on providing a theologate of 'Shorts' while waiting for a few more potential professors from their academic chrysalids must have seemed the better part of valour. So the 'Longs' crossed the narrow seas and seventeen students remained in St. Beuno's, being taught Moral by their new Rector, George Lambert, Dogma by Fr. Blackett for one year and Fr. Dykes the next, and learning about Scripture from James McSwiney. Fr. McSwiney was something of a Victorian polymath. He was later to teach Canon Law and acquire a formidable knowledge of both liturgical history and Celtic lore. As a youth in France he had learned Breton, a facility which served him well with Welsh converts.

In 1859 the 'Longs' men were regathered to the English Province's Welsh theologate and the effort to provide them with teachers resumed. The Rector continued to lecture in Moral Theology; Dogma was tackled by Fr. Porter and Fr. O'Callaghan and Canon Law by Fr. Whitty. Professor of Scripture was Henry Coleridge, old Etonian, former fellow of Oriel College, who seems to have been the first Jesuit that Hopkins ever met. Later, as Editor of 'The Month', Fr. Coleridge was to be offered the newly completed 'Wreck Of The Deutschland'. After scrutinising it diligently and in his ensuing bewilderment consulting one of Hopkins' contemporaries, he declined to publish a piece of which he himself could make nothing. In fairness to the dazed editor it has to be remembered that Robert Bridges on first reading the poem declared that he could not read it a second time 'for any money'.

In 1862 we find that continental Jesuits are once again shoring up the tottery structure, with Fr. Marocci (Rome) lecturing 'Shorts', the only foreigner, as far as I can see, ever to do so, and Fr. Bottala (Sicily) taking Church History. In the following year Fr. Bottala is listed as teaching Dogma, which he continued to do for nine years. Fr. Seed, who became Rector in 1864 broke with the tradition of teaching Moral as a sideline of that office. Fr. Harris, the hero of the 'Grand Act' taught the subject for one year, Fr. Lee for the succeeding year and Fr. Cardwell, the former Vice-Rector, kept the subject going for a further four years. During the second half of the 'sixties' the Short Course experienced a quite unusual period of stability, Fr. William Eyre taking the course for six consecutive years. Then, as if to compensate for this untypical equilibrium, in 1871 the 'Shorts' were abruptly and mysteriously transferred to Roehampton 'to edify the novices'. Whether the Beadle's tongue was buccally situated as he wrote down those four words, the Log cannot tell us. Autumn 1872 saw the future 'cabhorses' return to both St Beuno's and the habitual state of flux among their instructors. In the following nineteen years I count thirteen different men as succeeding one another in the post.

During Fr. Seed's rectorship St. Beuno's come to rely on imported continental talent only slightly less than it had done in its first years. Fr. Coleridge was succeeded in 1865 as Professor of Scripture by Fr. di Pietro (Sicily), Fr. Koerckemann and Fr. Duren (Germany) and then in 1872 by Fr. Perini (Venice) who persevered in the post for thirteen years. In the autumn of 1869 Fr. Bernard Tepe arrived to teach Dogma. This with a single year's break for his tertianship he was to do continuously until the summer of 1902. In that year he went, not back to Germany, but to the community of German Jesuits in exile at Valkenburg in Holland, where he became mortally ill. On Christmas Eve 1904 the morning post brought him a copy of theses defended in the end of term disputation at St. Beuno's. The dying man read through the list slowly and meticulously remarking from time to time, 'That's my thesis. I myself taught it. That's right'. Reassured that sound doctrine still prevailed at St. Beuno's, and would survive in the hands of his English successors, he finally added with a broad smile of satisfaction, 'Everything's all right at St. Beuno's. Nunc dimittis'. He died the same day.

In October 1871 Fr. Seed was replaced as Rector by Fr. Weld, who after only two years was summoned by the General, not to Rome, but to Fiesole, the seat of the exiled 'curia', to be his English Assistant. At St. Beuno's the post of Rector was then filled by Fr. James Jones, who was already Professor of Moral and therefore able to revive the traditional link between the two posts. When Gerard Manley Hopkins arrived for the academic year 1874-75 the Rector and Fr. John Morris, who taught Church History, were the only Englishmen among six lecturers. Dogma was taught by Frs. Tosi and Tepe, Scripture by Fr. Perini and the Short Course by Fr. Legnani. In Hopkins' second year Fr. Tosi was replaced by Fr. Floeck (Germany) and in the next year by Fr. Frins (Germany). Fr. Legnani also left in 1875 and 'Shorts' were put into the 'prentice hands of William Hayden, whose direct promotion from fourth year student to the staff is a pointed comment on the resources of the English Province.

One fact puzzles me. Among the thirty-odd Jesuits from other provinces who for longer or shorter periods taught at St. Beuno's I have spotted only three French names, and none of those remain on the lists for more than a year. Yet in 1879 there were roughly two French Jesuits for every Italian, four for every German and seven for every member of the English Province. Why did none of this abundance, or so little of it and for so very short a time flow in the direction of Tremeirchion, even when the French Jesuits were at Mold? The other question I ask myself without any evidence on which to build an answer, is how contented or resigned or ill at ease were these men from Italy and Germany perched on a Welsh hillside. Continental Jesuits were usually men of the city, trained in the towns, working in large centres of population, rubbing shoulders with both the wealthy and the miserably poor, breathing the same air as the devout and the fiercely anti-clerical, with every day bringing its own offering of political rumours and ecclesiastical gossip. 'I am in Ireland now; I am at a third remove'. Changing the fourth word to 'Wales', the exile from Rome or Venice or Cologne could make his own the verse his student would one day compose in Dublin. These men were out of their own country, separated from the members of their own Province and with so few contacts, if any, among the Welsh. Some of them did say mass at such centres as St. Asaph, where no doubt they struck the families of the Irish labourers and the Welsh converts as only a degree more foreign than the Lancashire-born or London-bred gentlemen who were St. Beuno's alternative offering. With what manner of conversation was the proverbial fly on the wall regaled when the seven (if Fr. Minister were present) members of the senior community of 1879 were gathered for their daily period of community recreation, and the three Englishmen, the three Italians and the single German, attempted a 'religiously agreeable and agreeably religious' causerie? Whatever the quality of their conversation in English, whether they were piously resigned to their sojourners' lot or more than content with the missionary role of providing heretical Britain with native Jesuit priests, there is no doubt that the English, now the British, Province owes a considerable debt to those involuntary expatriates who kept the English theologate afloat for almost forty years.

VIII

The poet and his peers

In Aug 1874 there arrived at St. Beuno's a man who was to lead to its being known (if often incorrectly prounouced) wherever English literature is comprehensively studied. When Gerard first glimpsed the house where his poetic genius would gather 'to a greatness like the ooze of oil crushed', it had already been standing for twenty-six years. During the first twenty of those years there had been few changes. In September 1849, the General, Fr. Roothaan, still one of '48's displaced persons, had visited the new theologate. To commemorate the occasion an oak was planted beside the building, and I have just this minute been outside to admire its present bulk, and then up on to the tower to judge its height. The oak is now taller than the tower. As well as the oak, Fr. Roothaan left behind him instructions that his visit should be remembered 'in perpetuum', not by some commemorative liturgy or scholastic display, but by a day's holiday to be celebrated in October. With the habitual tenacity of a religious community in the matter of its privileges, the theologians migrating to Oxfordshire in 1926 bore this holiday boon with them. I remember it as a very pleasant break, the first of the academic year. Also ascribed to Fr. Roothaan's visit to Britain is the instruction which was implemented at St. Beuno's on January 16th 1854, that all should 'mount the Roman collar'. The General is said to have been quite taken aback on arrival to see his welcoming party in brown overcoats and 'chokers'. When at St. Beuno's on September 19th 1941 I 'mounted' my first Roman collar, I did so quite unaware that in Britain the use of such objects was less than a century old. Now, I can say to anyone enquiring somewhat censoriously why I am not wearing a Roman collar, that, having as a history teacher acquired a strong sense of tradition, I regard the article, introduced in the middle of the nineteenth century, as a new-fangled imposition.

The years after the General's visit saw the Chapel set to rights, the Rock Chapel Field purchased and its shrine built, and the

photogenic stone stairway constructed which soars to the topmost
terrace. The first considerable development came in the Rectorship
of Fr. Alfred Weld. Fr. Weld was a man of experience and
decision. He had been a novicemaster at thirty-seven, Provincial at
forty-one and after two years at St. Beuno's was to be elevated to
the position of English Assistant. In those two years he altered the
fabric more than any of his predecessors or successors. With the
number of students now hovering near forty, he decided that
additional rooms were needed, and he supplied them on quite a
scale. A new wing was added to the north of the tower. This
extension provided at basement level two lecture rooms, on the
floor above a Recreation Room for the 'Fathers', i.e. the senior
community, and three professors' rooms, and on the top floor ten
students rooms. Because of the poem 'Moonrise', in which the
poet sees the moon touching 'dark Maenefa the mountain', it is
conjectured that Hopkins had one of the five new rooms facing
the hillside. Thirteen additional living rooms did not satisfy Fr.
Weld. Five rooms were fitted into the space under the roof on the
west side, where a passage runs from the tower to the Chapel
Gallery. They were later called Tower Hamlets. Five more rooms
were similarly inserted beneath the roof on the south side at the
very top of the house and came to be called Attica. Most of these
ten rooms, so ingeniously contrived, were judged to be 'so tiny
and comfortless' that on the completion of the work they were
found to be 'scarcely habitable'. Certainly, in comparison with the
generously proportioned rooms on the Chapel Gallery and above,
they seem to have been designed for a smaller race of beings.
Some of the new quarters had central heating which spared their
occupants the daily chore of clearing out the ashes and resetting.
However, if G.M.H. is echoing general opinion, those still with
fires were held to be better off, smoke, cinders and ashes not-
withstanding. 'Pipes of affliction convey lukewarm water of affliction to some of the rooms, others more fortunate have fires'.

Fr. Weld, no doubt, judged that an expanding Province required
a theologate of increased capacity and this he had provided, partly
by building a new wing, but also, more frugally, by exploiting the
remaining spaces in the old building. The work was complete
when G.M.H. arrived. The Province was certainly growing. At the
beginning of the year 1848 there had been 86 priests and 74
scholastics; early in 1874 there were 173 priests and 139 scholas-

tics. Not that there was any slack. There were now five developing colleges; the Province had spread into Scotland, where there
were seventeen men; the city parishes teemed; there were men
working in Guiana, Honduras and Jamaica, while seven Englishmen served under French or German or Belgian superiors in India.
It is pleasant to record that, in spite of this pressure, the year
which brought G.M.H. to St. Beuno's had taken Fr. Perry and Fr.
Sidgreaves across the Roaring Forties to Kerguelen, or the Isle of
Desolation, to study the transit of Venus across the sun. In July
'75 Fr. Perry would visit St. Beuno's so that Hopkins and his
fellow students could hear his adventures and observations from
his own mouth.

In the academic year 1874-75 G.M.H. was one of fourteen first
year students. In the Province catalogue they are quaintly arranged
in the alphabetical order of the Latin versions of their first name,
but with 'Longs' taking due precedence over 'Shorts'. The first
therefore to be named is Albert Wagner, who in spite of that most
Teutonic of names, was a member of the Lyons Province. The
second name is that of Charles Morrogh, like George Kelly, the
sixth name, a member of the Irish Province. Gerard's other
companions were of the home Province. Cyprian Splaine had been
born into a Liverpool family which was to give three of its four
sons to the Society. After leaving Stonyhurst he had joined the
noviceship in 1863 when almost twenty years of age. He later
taught for five years at his old school before coming to St.
Beuno's, where he proved to be a good moral theologian, an
excellent Latinist and the most assiduous member of a group
which met three times a week to carry their Hebrew beyond the
level acquired in the statutory course. One would like to know
whether G.M.H. was a member of this zealous circle, or whether
he was too occupied with Scotus or Welsh verse forms.

Frederick Hopkins had been born in Birmingham in 1844 and
educated by the Rosminians at Ratcliffe. He spent some time in
the seminary at Oscott, but left, qualified in medicine and practised it until, with another change of direction, he joined the
novitiate in 1868 on the same day as his namesake. He taught for
a year at Mount St. Mary's before starting theology, his fellow theologians labelling him 'the genteel Hop.' because of his
continuing bedside manner, whereas Gerard became 'the gentle
Hop.'. Frederick put his medical knowledge at the disposal of his

brethren with 'unfailing charity, attention and skill', and when the Rector, Fr. Jones, decided to economise by putting out the fire in the Recreation Room, the doctor-theologian insisted that the health of the community was suffering as a result. Impressed by expert knowledge, the Rector relented and this very parsimonious sounding economy was revoked. William Dubberley, born in Monmouth in 1843, was a Stonyhurst boy who entered the novitiate in 1862 and taught for six years, one at Stonyhurst, five at Beaumont, before reaching theology. William Splaine, almost three years younger than his brother Cyprian, was less able academically and joined the Society only in 1866. He taught briefly at both Beaumont and Stonyhurst. Hugh Ryan was born in Limerick in 1843 but educated at Oscott. He returned to Ireland to study at Trinity College, but left after two and a half years without graduating. He entered the English Province in 1865 and saw his share of teaching at Liverpool.

Joseph Rickaby's father was butler to William Constable-Maxwell, later Baron Herries. Joseph was born in 1845 and became the playmate of his employer's second son, William. When William was told that he must soon follow his elder brother to Stonyhurst, he vehemently refused to be parted from Joe. His parents, solution to this impasse was to send both their son and the butler's son to Stonyhurst, and Joe's young brother John after them. The future Lord Herries had backed two winners. Both Joe and John raked in the prizes and showed every promise of intellectual distinction. Joseph became a novice in 1862 and by 1870 had completed his philosophy course while securing an M.A. degree. His London examiners declared him a brilliant examinee and his papers of exceptional quality. For four years he prepared the Secular Philosophers of Stonyhurst for the B.A. course and then entered St. Beuno's before his twenty-ninth birthday. Stephen Hayes, born of Irish parents in 1843, was another Stonyhurst boy. He entered the noviceship in 1863, took a London B.A. degree while studying philosophy, and saw service in the classrooms of both Beaumont and Stonyhurst. Sydney Smith, born in 1843, was the son of an Evangelical Anglican clergyman. At the age of eighteen, having no wish to follow his father, but being in his own words, 'on the verge of atheism', he was sent to London to enter his grandfather's firm of architects. He had the good fortune to lodge with a devout 'High Church' family, and under their influence became genuinely interested in religious matters for the first time. A period of assiduous reading, discussion and church visiting led him in 1864 to be received as a Catholic by Fr. Christie of Farm Street, whom we last saw crossing France in the company of his 'workgirls'. He entered the Society two years later and was on the staff at Stonyhurst before coming to St. Beuno's. Then there are the two 'Shorts' men, Austin Marchant and Clement Barraud. Concerning Austin Marchant, who was to leave the Society in 1881, information is scarce. Born in 1843, he was a Londoner who came to the novitiate in 1869. He taught for one year in Liverpool and another at Stonyhurst. Clement Barraud, born in 1843, was of Huguenot origin. Losing his father at the age of eight, he was adopted by a Catholic convert uncle, but did not himself become a Catholic for several years. He then spent two years at Stonyhurst, leaving there to work as a stained glass artist for three years, before becoming a Jesuit novice in 1862. His scholasticate was unusually peripatetic, taking him into the class-rooms of four different colleges before he reached theology.

Of the eleven members of the English Province brought together in 1874 six had been born in 1843 and three in 1844. Only William Splaine and Joseph Rickaby were not yet thirty. Was thirty considered to be the optimum age at which the apprentice Jesuit should begin to court the Queen of the Sciences? Or were the expanding colleges, whose part in the early career of these men I have carefully noted, already exerting a leech-like thirst for young blood? I suspect the latter to be the more important factor. One thing is clear, that 'the gentle Hop.' had been very gently treated in this respect. While his peers had faced the 'sharp and sided hail' which can fly in any schoolroom, he had spent a year 'out of the swing of the sea' teaching the Jesuit Juniors, as tractable a species of male pupil as could be found anywhere in Britain. The eleven of '74, like the class of '49, consisted largely of Stonyhurst pupils with a few converts but with the admixture of two cradle Catholics from Oscott. But if the past of Hopkins' peers resembles that of their predecessors twenty-five years before, several of them were destined to deploy their priesthood in quite different circumstances from those of Albany Christie and Co.

Cyprian Splaine, admired at St. Beuno's for his Latinity, found himself teaching the senior class at Stonyhurst and preparing them for their London Examination. His contemporaries blamed his 'unflagging assiduity' in this post for the collapse in health which made him an invalid as early as 1887 and brought him to his death five years later at the age of forty-nine. Frederick Hopkins, 'the genteel Hop.' having been Minister in the noviceship house for some years, sailed in 1887 to Honduras, where eleven years later he became the Bishop. In April 1923 he was travelling with three nuns in a Nothern Mail boat which was carrying too many passengers and too much luggage and began to take in water. This it continued to do for some hours, finally sinking in eighteen feet of water. The Bishop and two of the nuns, one of whom had given her lifebelt to a man with a wife and family ashore, were drowned in what could pass for a remake of 'The Wreck Of The Deutschland'. The genteel Hop.'s decomposing body floated ashore in Yucatan, was hastily interred, later exhumed and buried solemnly in Belize. 'During the funeral services, the Government Offices and all stores and shops were closed' in tribute. The Bishop was seventy-nine. William Dubberley spent seventeen years in Liverpool where he was responsible for the domestic arrangements of the house, supervised the church services, organised the parish schools and did his share of parish visiting, being particularly welcomed by the children. He had a high reputation as a school administrator, was much sought after as a retreat giver, but was admired above all for his carefully prepared and very effective preaching. He died of typhoid in 1896 aged fifty-two. William Splaine also spent his priesthood in parish work spending more than twenty years at Preston. He died at St. Helen's aged sixty-six 'at work up to the very end'. Hugo Ryan sailed east to help the Jesuits of the Turin Province at Mangalore, where he fell ill and died quite abruptly at the age of forty-six. Joseph Rickaby was to be one of the best known Jesuits of his time. He taught Ethics at St. Mary's Hall until 1896, when he went to Oxford where he gave conferences to the students, being also invited regularly to Cambridge and quite frequently to Oscott. At Oscott he gave addresses to the seminarists and was their spiritual counsellor. His talks and his sermons could rivet equally schoolboys, Lancashire villagers and his fellow scholars. His writings gained him a national reputation and were quoted for decades after his death. He wrote on philosophical topics, on Scripture and Ascetical Theology. He took a special satisfaction in his 'Index To The Works Of Newman', and provided a new translation of 'The

Spiritual Exercises' and of Rodriguez' classic work 'Perfection and Christian Virtue'. He wrote fifty-eight articles for 'The Month' alone. Frail as he had always appeared, he lived to be eighty-seven, dying at St. Beuno's in 1932.

Stephen Hayes after his ordination taught for twenty-two years, holding such important positions as Prefect of Studies at Mount St. Mary's, Prefect of the Lay Philosophers at Stonyhurst and Superior of the Jesuit Juniors. He took leave of the classroom in 1902, working in the parishes of Edinburgh, Clitheroe and Glasgow. He died at St. Mary's Hall at the age of seventy-nine. Sydney Smith, the clergyman's son, was patently a man of intellectual capacity, but it took some years for him to find his métier. Returning to St. Beuno's in 1883 he took the Short Course for a year, Dogma for a second and taught Scripture for four years after that. In 1889 he was sent to Wimbledon then moved on to Farm Street two years later. He was to remain there till 1921. He worked on 'The Month', writing a great deal himself on Church history and doctrine. Much of his work was penned in what we would consider a polemical vein, but his vigorous style seems to have suited the period and did not prevent him being an early ecumenist and a frequent guest speaker at the meetings of The Society of St. Thomas of Canterbury. A good deal of his time went in instructing converts, preaching retreats and giving spiritual counsel. He died in 1922 aged seventy-nine. Austin Marchant after a few years at Great Yarmouth left the Society during 1881. Clement Barraud was despatched in 1880 to Georgetown, Guiana. He taught in St. Stanislaus College and worked in the local church. In the oppressive, humid coastal heat he still found the energy to write dramas, compose music and edit a paper. He was moved in 1900 to a lonely and exacting mission on Barbados. Returning to Britain in 1909, he was appointed Spiritual Father at St. Beuno's where he died in 1926 at eighty-three.

When the First Year students took their places at the opening lectures in October 1874 they were all of much the same age, had undergone the same formation and had the same purpose, to equip themselves as priests of the Society. To what very different ends that priesthood would bring them: William Dubberley and 'the gentle Hop.' to die of typhoid in large cities, Hugh Ryan coughing up pieces of his windpipe in Mangalore, the putrifying corpse of 'the genteel Hop.' cast up on the sands of Corozal, and others breathing their last as revered old gentlemen in houses of formation, Sydney Smith in the noviceship, Stephen Hayes among the Philosophers, and two, Joe Rickaby and Clement Barraud surrounded by another generation in St. Beuno's itself. Much of my information about these men is drawn from their obituaries, which always have a tendency to eulogise. Even making generous allowance for that kindly bias, there seems to be one quality undeniably common to all. They all exhibit a diligence, a zeal, a highly developed, even at times over-developed, sense of responsibility. Fr. Dubberley's preaching had to be restricted by his Superior because he took on 'an incredible number of sermons away from home'. Cyprian Splaine shortened his life through his 'unflagging assiduity'. G.M.H. agonised over a complex system of half and even quarter marks which he had invented, lest he do some student faintly less than justice. Bishop Hopkins was described as 'giving no thought to self, to comfort or to his age . . . even when there were missionary journeys that tried the endurance of strong young men'. William Splaine was 'at work till the end'. The same drive was behind the innumerable sermons, lectures, conferences and multifarious writings of Frs. Rickaby and Smith. These men—(with the possible exception of Austin Marchant)—were good priests. Fr. Lythgoe could rest content.

The decade which followed the advent of G.M.H. in 1874 establishes something of a plateau in the development of St. Beuno's as a theologate. In 1874-75 Gerard had been one of thirty-eight students. By 1884-5 the number had reached fifty-two, a total which would never be exceeded. With that many students, the staff and thirteen brothers, the house had to accommodate seventy-four people. As there have never been that many private rooms in the building, I suspect that a number of brothers slept in some form of dormitory over the refectory. I have slept there more than once as a novice in 1941, when our numbers had again caused the house almost to overflow. The other change during this ten years was towards the indigenisation and stabilisation of the staff. Stabilisation comes first with even the continental Jesuits less likely to flit in and out of the teaching posts. Fr. Perini, having taught Dogma during 1871-2, then lectured in Scripture for the next thirteen years. Fr. Tepe, as we have seen more than doubled that record, coming in '69 and leaving in 1902. The significant event of the decade 1874-84 was the appointment in 1880 of John

Rickaby, Joe's brother, to teach Dogma, the first Englishman to do
so since '68. At first he taught the subject for only three years,
being sent back to St. Mary's Hall to lecture in Logic and General
Metaphysics. He returned eight years later and resumed his chair
in Dogma for a further eleven years. The eight years of his
absence were covered, not by some German or Italian refugee, but
by Fr. O'Fallon-Pope, who, in spite of his American mother, was a
genuine member of the English Province. The students who
experienced the changeover from Fr. Rickaby to Fr. O'Fallon-Pope
or the reversal in '91 must have been at least temporarily bewildered by the contrast of styles. John Rickaby stressed the historical
element and showed how rigid, a priori formulae needed to be
modified when that factor was properly taken into account. He
made his pupils aware that their textbooks did not have the
infallibility that their tone seemed to claim, that there was a good
deal to be said against the theses which were stated so authorita-
tively, and he often seemed to cast doubt on whether certainty were possible at all when all aspects of the matter had
been weighed. He was playful, unsystematic and eclectic. Fr.
O'Fallon-Pope was at the opposite pole, utterly rigid, undeviat-
ingly Scholastic in his opinions and wholly uninterested in other
views and approaches. The curious aspect of this situation was
that Rickaby was a cradle Catholic and educated entirely by and in
the Society since the age of thirteen, whereas O'Fallon-Pope was a
convert and a graduate of Christ Church, who had studied
philosophy with the Benedictines and theology at Rome, joining
the Society when he was already a priest.

Fr. James Jones, who was Rector during G.M.H.'s first two
years, had taught Moral Theology for six years when he left in '76
to become Provincial. In 1880 he was appointed Rector for a
second time and also resumed teaching Moral. The most significant fact here is that when Fr. Hunter became Rector in 1885,
Fr. Jones continued to teach Moral for another seven years,
notching up a total of seventeen years before handing over to Fr.
Thomas Slater. 'Moral' had ceased to be a side activity of the
Rector's and was, along with Dogma, attaining some sort of
continuity in its teaching. When Fr. Perini left in '85 his place as
Professor of Scripture was taken by Fr. Sydney Smith, whom we
met among Hopkins' classmates. He was replaced in '89 by
Herbert Lucas who would continue in the post until 1902. When

G.M.H. started theology four of the staff were foreign. Eleven years later all but Tepe belong to the home Province. Twenty years later Tepe and Rickaby are teaching Dogma, Slater both Moral and Canon Law and Lucas Scripture. All four men are experienced; all four will stay for several years. The situation is now professional and stable—except, of course, for those academic Cinderellas, or should I say, trainee cabhorses, in Shorts, who have between '94 and '99 four different teachers.

The three years which Gerard Manley Hopkins spent at St. Beuno's saw in him a double metamorphosis. In December '75 the tragedy of 'The Deutschland' and his Rector's remark that someone should write a poem about the event, stirred the blue-bleak embers of his self-imposed silence to gall themselves and gash the gold-vermilion of his most celebrated poem. September '77 witnessed the long prepared for three day eclosion from the chrysalid of the Jesuit scholastic to the newly ordained priest of the Church. Every admirer of the poet needs to realise that for Gerard himself it was the second event which mattered the more. Early in 1848, when St. Beuno's was a-building the English Province contained 86 priests. At the beginning of 1878, with Hopkins among their number, they mustered 200. That background is not to be omitted as we contemplate the priesting of the poet.

IX

Drains, Brains and Bedesmen

St. Beuno's was a theologate from 1848 till 1926, a period of seventy-eight years. When G.M.H. left in 1877, not staying for his fourth year, there were still forty-nine of those years to run. They are, at least on the surface, placid years. Numbers settled down about the mid eighties, and except for a minor crisis in 1902, the lecturing was more or less on an even keel. The changes which took place in the building itself were comparatively superficial. By 1880 four altars, two of them very solid, imposing but looming somewhat Brobdingnagian in their narrow settings, had been erected in the passage leading from the organ tribune towards the north. In 1906 a block of lavatories was added on the south east side 'in the interests of health'. Hygienic it may have been, chiefly, I should think, because any germs perished quickly from the cold. It was a barn of a place with fourteen cubicles, quite separate from the house and without any heating. Even the four handbasins ran only with cold water. One went to it across a nine foot bridge, known to us novices as the Bridge of Sighs, because there was a ten inch gap between the side walls and the roof. On a wintry day the razor-edged draught almost took one's head off, and made the unwarmed area beyond seem quite cosy in comparison. When I came back to the house as a tertian some indulgent minister had taken the sybaritic step of filling in the gap with glass, so sparing us this brief Spartan ordeal.

In 1909 the then Minister, Fr. Dobson, trebled the number of baths available by adding two more to the one and only specimen which had for so long served a community sometimes exceeding seventy. What preoccupied the authorities during the nineteenth century was the chilliness of much of the house, particularly in the Hamlets and Attica where the draughts ran riot. They also worried about the uncertainty of the water supply in the summer months. "What if we have a fire during a dry summer?", someone would ask. This disconcerting query was met by a scheme to provide a sizeable reservoir dug in the hillside above the terraces, and so provide not only a reliable head of water, but also a swimming pool. The excavation duly took place but, with money even shorter than summer water, the resulting broad, deep hollow was never puddled and never connected with the hill springs. This afternoon I clambered through the brambles and spring nettles, the planted conifers and the self-sown saplings to locate the site. I finally came upon it, a wide and once deep hole hideous with accumulated rubbish, which included several corpse-white plastic chemical containers, several large rolls of rusting wire and the chassis of two cars.

If my trip to the reservoir/swimming pool planned, begun and abandoned, was somewhat depressing, it was a good deal less poignant than the imaginary journey suggested and rejected by an anonymous obituarist in 1934: 'In this connexion it does not seem necessary to retrace the steps which Fr. Lucas trod with so much personal pain and sense of failure and defeat'. Herbert Lucas was the first boy from Beaumont College to enter the Society, which he did in 1869. As a scholastic he prepared the Stonyhurst Lay Philosophers for London degrees, and while doing so, took an M.A. in Classics and Philosophy, achieving the first place and the prize in Philosophy and the second place in Classics. His obvious brilliance marked him out as professorial material, and he was sent to Rome for further studies in Scripture, which he then taught at St. Beuno's from 1889 to 1901. He was therefore dealing with the subject as the so-called Modernist movement gathered momentum and ecclesiastical authority began to react with what was in the end paranoiac repressiveness. Fr. Lucas, no-one could rationally suspect of unorthodoxy, but, 'he was torn between his loyalty to authority and his conception of the adequate teaching which should be afforded to the students . . . Fr. Lucas stood for the general principle of "opening doors and windows, and admitting plenty of fresh air".' He endured this painful situation until 1901. Did he leave because he had fallen under suspicion? Not necessarily. He had lectured for twelve years, and that was by previous standards quite a stint. On the other hand, the fact that the gap had to be filled by once more calling in foreign talent makes one wonder. Fr. Deimel of Germany filled in for two years, and then Fr. Fernandez of Aragon for three, until the arrival of Charles Townsend in 1906. Meanwhile Fr. Lucas deployed his zeal elsewhere, at Liverpool, Worcester and Liverpool again, until he died at eighty-three. One Worcester story deserves to be told. 'He had gone on foot immediately after mass, fasting, to take Communion to an aged couple at Martley Workhouse, eight miles away. This done, he breakfasted off a twopenny meat pie and a banana, washing it down with some water from a brook. Feeling refreshed, he hunted up the Catholics of the countryside, and returned home, walking, to dinner'. At the time he was approaching seventy.

Fr. Lucas's painful internal conflicts are unlikely to have found any echo in the legal mind of Fr. Thomas Slater. Thomas, who had been a boy at Mount St. Mary's and then Stonyhurst, was ordained in 1888. He was then sent to Rome to study Canon Law and Ecclesiastical History, the chair in those subjects having been vacant since 1882. Returning to St. Beuno's in 1892, he was asked, in the absence of Fr. Jones at the General Congregation, to take Moral Theology. Then Fr. Jones fell ill during the Congregation and died, so that the emergency of 1892-3 was prolonged for another eighteen years, Fr. Slater shouldering the teaching of Moral until his degenerating eyesight compelled him to retire. His lack of training for the post of Moral Theology he strove to remedy by intensive preparation of his lectures, spending even the Long Vacation in laborious study. His teaching was, of course, affected both by his canonical studies and his academic method of preparation and was somewhat legalistic and bookish. However, when he left St. Beuno's, he went to St. Francis Xavier's, Liverpool and spent very long hours in the confessional, hearing as many as 31,000 confessions in a year, drawing people of all classes from all over the city. Presumably his confessional practice was of a very different complexion from his lecture room presentation. In spite of persistent eye trouble he produced a two-volume 'Moral Theology' in English, which sold well on both sides of the Atlantic.

Very different in character yet again from both Fr. Lucas and Fr. Slater, was John Jaggar, who arrived on the staff in 1889 and was to teach continuously until 1925. His father was a High Church town official in Wakefield, whose wife, together with the twelve year old John, became a Catholic in 1874. John was then sent to Mount St. Mary's, from which he joined the Society. Ordained in 1895 he spent a year at Wimbledon College as Prefect of Studies before starting to lecture in Dogmatic Theology without any additional studies in the subject. (I am beginning to regret my word 'professional', used in the last chapter of the teaching situation at this period. It can be justified only in comparison with the ramshackle expedients of an earlier time). For five years Fr. Jaggar taught the Short Course, his predecessor having done so for two years and the man before him for one. He was promoted to the Longs Course in 1903 and lectured until a year before the move to Heythrop in 1926. He studied unremittingly, claiming to have worked his way through all the Latin Fathers and many of the Greeks. His reading of the Latin Fathers did not greatly benefit his own spoken Latin, which gave some amusement to the more classically competent of his audience. In the 5,000 lectures which it is calculated that he delivered there was more than a flavour of Sacred Eloquence. On one occasion as an even more declamatory address than usual reached its plangent conclusion, one wag on the benches firmly intoned the 'Credo In unum Deum' which follows the sermon at a High Mass. The ten years which remained to him after leaving St. Beuno's were spent giving—which in those days meant preaching—retreats and giving conferences to a wide variety of folk including the Apostolic Union of Priests and the 'Zita Confraternity Of Servant Girls' in Upper Belgrave St.

Fr. Philip St. John I should like to mention because my heart warms to him. His father was a Baptist minister whose wife, like that of Mr. Jaggar, became a Catholic, but this time with two sons, Stanislaus and Philip, Philip being ten years old. The boys were sent to France for their schooling and joined the English noviceship together in 1884. As a scholastic Philip taught 'Preparatory' and was remarkably successful. 'He had a great insight into the mind of the small boy, and a manner they could easily interpret'. Paying much more attention than usual to peda-gogic flair, superiors had him 'marked down for a future Dogmatic Professor'. He prepared for this office at Valkenburg and at Rome before coming to St. Beuno's in 1904. He took the Short Course and taught them with 'a power of lucid expression and an almost infinite care to learn the point of view of his auditors'. 'Shorts' had the services of this model teacher for eleven years, doubtless a golden era in the history of that ill-served section of the theologate. In 1915 he was withdrawn and not replaced. In 1914 the number of lecturers had risen to the unprecedented number of seven with the addition of a lecturer in Fundamental Theology, Fr.

Leonard Geddes, who had spent two years additional theological studies among the exiled French at Hastings. It was the wrong time for expansion. The Great War needed chaplains, which meant gaps in the schools and parishes. Fr. St. John went off, not to the Front but to Manchester and a succession of parish appointments including, I am glad to say, six years with his brother Stanislaus at Wardour.

In telling the story of a theologate it is easily done to focus on those who provided the theology, and to lose sight of those who provided food, fuel and clothes and saw to the maintenance and cleaning of the house which sheltered both teachers and taught. During vacations there are weeks without a single lecture; there cannot be a day without meals or a week without cleaning, while the wear and tear to the fabric of either the building or the residents' clothes is a constant factor. All these things fell within the sphere of the Minister, who co-ordinated the work of the laybrothers and the hired servants. Perusing the list of the men who held that office at St. Beuno's I am taken aback by the rapid turnover. In the first thirty-one years of the house there were twenty-two appointments. Between 1870 and 1879, which, of course, covers the period of Hopkins' residence, there was a new Minister each year. In the eighties and nineties there is more stability, with only three men covering the period 1880 to 1892, just as there is more continuity during this period in the teaching of Dogma, Moral and Scripture. However, with the first decade of the twentieth century it was back to the merry-go-round with five ministers in five years, and eight between 1899 and 1908. It is intriguing that during the same decade there was a similar fit of hiccups in the lecturing, when the house had to be bailed out once more by the continental refugees, Frs. Deimel, Cladder, Gonthier, Taafe and Fernandez.

Such brevity of tenure in a not unimportant office meant that living conditions depended even more than they should have done on the willingness and competence of the brothers. It was their cooking and mending, cleaning and nursing which sustained the life of the community. In the early years of the house there were usually half-a-dozen brothers, a generous apportionment for a handful of lecturers and about twenty-five students. In the seventies, as the student body pushed towards fifty, the number of brothers came up to about ten or eleven. During the eighties there were in addition two or three brothers whose names in the lists are marked 'cur. val', infirm old men, beyond active work, who may have needed a good deal of care from the infirmarian. The contribution of such old brothers to the life of the community, in spite of their physical inactivity, was of the highest value because it was in the sphere which gave the house its point. It lay in their simplicity, their undemandingness but especially in their prayers, which were long, heartfelt, uncomplicated and direct. Prayer flowed from the physically withered landscape of their lives like the stream at the foot of the glacier, constant and unconstrained.

One brother who worked to prepare the College for its opening in 1848 came back to it to die. This was Joseph Mero, born in Naples in 1807, who joined the Naples Province in 1827. On one occasion in his younger days he had been lent to a papal official, Monsignor Joachim Pecci, who needed to be nursed through a severe fever. The Monsignor recovered and later became Pope Leo XIII. I am at a loss to know what qualifications as a nurse, other than dutifulness, Brother Mero had, because he was a carpenter by trade. It was in that capacity that he left fine specimens of his work in Calcutta, Malta and several English Province houses. In community he was lively company, shrewd, original and humorous. For almost the last ten years of his life, which were spent at St. Beuno's, he was totally blind. He died, aged eighty, from cancer of the tongue, throughout which illness he bore himself 'patient and resigned to the end'. During his dark years the practical phlegmatic English scholastics, when faced with examinations, were in the habit of going to Brother Mero to ask for his prayers. Brother Mero would enquire the precise time of the exam, and, when the day and the hour came, make his way to the Chapel, there to tell his beads until the crisis was past. In this diptych of the sightless brother confidently praying and the apprentice theologian stammering out his exposition and hoping that his formulae and his answers are correct, do I have a parable of the relationship between Christian prayer and academic Theology?

Brother Michael Goodge, who arrived in the early days of the College and served it unbrokenly for twenty-five years, was an Irishman, born in Dublin on the day of Waterloo. He joined the English Province in 1842. He was a tailor. As his time at St.

Beuno's overlapped with that of G.M.H. by one year, he might have made the still silent poet a gown or suit, or more likely repaired a rent received on some nature ramble. One job, I am sorry to say, which Brother Goodge performed every morning for a quarter of a century was to go round the rooms 'emptying slops', a chore performed, I hope, only for the senior Fathers. He went from St. Beuno's to Roehampton, the novitiate. With all the novices to be put into black suits and gowns on their vow day and the Juniors to be kept decently clad, there was plenty to do. He died in 1886.

James McKeon was also Irish born, migrating to Liverpool with his two brothers, all three practising the trade of plasterers. In 1865 the brothers attended a parish mission, as a result of which the whole trio entered the Society. James was sent to St. Beuno's, helping in the house generally, and from 1872-80 was responsible for the refectory. From 1881-85 he had charge under the Novicemaster of the brother novices. From 1886 he was Assistant Accountant at Stonyhurst until in 1895 he went to Wimbledon, where the College had just begun. 'In those now distant days Brother James was invaluable. With Br. W. James as cook and himself as factotum, the two ran Wimbledon'. He died there in 1925. When Br. McKeon was refectorian at St. Beuno's did G.M.H., with his love of traditional craft terms and phrases, pick up any interesting words from the Irish ex-plasterer, or from the blind carpenter who joined the community for Gerard's last year? Did his poet's ear mark down any intriguing speech rhythms in the conversation of the Irish born Liverpudlian or of the venerable, much travelled Neapolitan?

The poet probably never met Br. Patrick Welch, who only entered the Society in 1879, being then seventeen. In spite of his name he was a thoroughgoing Londoner. He came to St. Beuno's in 1881, helped in the house and in the refectory and then did similar work in London for nine years. Returning to St. Beuno's in 1905, he is listed as 'cur. val' i.e. 'on the sick list', but recovered to become sacristan in 1910. That position he held till 1926, the year of the migration to Heythrop, dying in 1927. Those are the 'salient facts' of his life, which leave out all the important things such as 'the tone and charm of his spoken word . . . the cheerfulness and serenity that comes from a deep and childlike confidence in God . . . His unfailing example of contented service'. Most relevant to us: 'Brother Pat was an indispensable part of the homeliness of St. Beuno's'.

Brother William McKay was another 'character' in the folk history of St. Beuno's. Liverpool saw his birth on Christmas Eve, 1854. He became a 'printer's machineman' before entering the Society in 1879. He worked at the Roehampton Press for a couple of years and came to St. Beuno's in 1884, first to help in the refectory but later being recorded as 'lithographer'. He was ill during the year 1893-94 and on his recovery was made assistant infirmarian, and after that refectorian until 1909. In that year he was transferred to Stonyhurst where he was again an infirmarian, dying there in 1938. Lithographer, refectorian and infirmarian! Obviously the brothers, or some of them, were expected to be as versatile as some of the early professors. It is a relief to read that Brother McKay 'was noted for his kind treatment and close attention to cases of serious illness', and that he 'could be as gentle as a woman, and his nursing was wonderfully skilful'. Perhaps his patients also benefited from his sense of humour, as he had 'a most irresistibly funny manner', while 'His sayings, of course, were famous'.

In 1904 George Tyrrell, perhaps the most intellectually gifted and certainly the most controversial of St. Beuno's former students, wrote a long letter to Fr. Martin, the General. It is a blistering indictment of the Society, occupying twenty pages of smallish print. One of his last points concerns 'his abhorrence of the treatment meted out to the laybrothers of the Society'. He charges the Society with having taken in young men to do menial work, deliberately keeping them in a state of 'blank ignorance' and yet demanding 'the psychological feat of an hour's meditation every morning and two quarters of self-introspection in the course of the day'. Then, 'nothing is to be done for his mind or for the development of his intelligence. He is to work like a dog in a mill, year in and year out . . . he has no prospects, no career before him; no work that grows'.

My five St. Beuno's brothers were not selected with an eye to refuting Tyrrell. I chose Br. Mero because he helped to prepare the theologate for its opening, the other four because of their long service to it. None of them give the impression of having been reduced to dull nonentities or of suffering from spiritual destitution, which is not to say that their lives wholly invalidate Tyrrell's charges. Tyrrell himself, not the man to ignore evidence, admitted, 'Numbers of laybrothers I have known who put us priests to shame in a thousand ways'. I have emphasised that many of the brothers were men of prayer. I personally doubt that they owed this facility to the excellence of their noviceship instruction, and I do not believe that it came from any subsequent guidance. I suggest that it sprang, under grace, from their own faith and goodwill and was confirmed by the dedication of many of the priests whom they supported and even sustained by their work. The legislation of the Society declares that brothers are to be treated with 'due love and reverence, as brothers and fellow workers in the Lord and sons of the same Society'. Where such respect and consideration was given, the idealism which had brought the brother to the noviceship and seen him through it, could blossom into the robust, selfless dedication which so many of them achieved. Unfortunately the swelling parishes, the developing colleges, the expanding missions overseas, with a background of Victorian industrialism, easily created a climate in which Brothers, teaching scholastics, and even priests could be thought of as tools, and their personal and spiritual needs be ignored. In such a situation it was the brothers who were the most exposed.

How did they fare at St. Beuno's? In a theologate the scholastics, so soon to be priests, would have had first place in the Rector's mind, whilst the 'senior Fathers, who shared his responsibilities, lived near him and sat at his end of the dining-room, could hardly be overlooked'. The Brothers I suspect came a poor third. On the other hand, they were numerous enough to form a community of their own and the theologians being birds of passage, even if it was a slow four-year passage, were less part of the place than the brother who had been some years in the house, and had his individual responsibility. Surviving anecdotes and vignettes give the impression of a cheerful, humorous relationship between students and laybrothers, of a relaxed interpretation of the 'rule of communities'. Whether this amounted to the rule's 'due love and reverence' I am not sure. Of one thing I am quite certain. Without the brothers the theologate could not have survived. Whatever the priests of the English Province achieved by their retreat-giving, teaching, preaching, writing, in Britain and overseas, was in part made possible by the work of the brothers.

The 'sheer plod' of their lives helped the 'plough down sillion' in college, parish and mission not only to shine, but to bring on the harvest, in which the 'hurrahs' would rarely be for them.

The kitchen entrance, portcullis and all

X

*The chair of Moses
and the Provincial's table*

It was not any conscious intention of implementing the gospel
precept 'the first shall be last' which has led to my speaking of the
laybrothers who worked in the theologate before the rectors who
presided over it. Many of the latter have been mentioned in the
course of the narrative, and I should now like to pass them briefly
in review, to observe what variations occurred among the species
and see whether there is any evolution at work.

The first Rector, Fr. John Etheridge (1848-51) was born in 1811
and had entered the Society before he was seventeen. He had
made his own theological studies at Louvain, where he had
performed the 'Grand Act'. He was then successively, in the
way of those pre-specialists times, Prefect of Lower Studies at
Stonyhurst, Professor of Logic to the Philosophers and a missioner
at St. Helens. He taught Theology for one year at the old
seminary at Stonyhurst before becoming the first Rector of the
new theologate at the age of thirty-seven, and with no previous
experience as a superior. It was the sort of thing which happened
in a Province which had eighty-six priests. That he made quite a
good fist of the job seems clear from the fact that three years later
he became Provincial. He was plainly a man of calibre. Attending
the General Congregation in 1853 he was chosen to be the English
Assistant to the General, which gave him oversight of the Jesuits
of England, Ireland, Maryland and Missouri. St. Beuno's had not
done badly in its first Rector.

The post stayed in the family. The next Rector was James
Etheridge (1851-55), three years John's senior. He had been a
bright pupil at school—Stonyhurst, of course—but had not been
employed in any academic post. He had worked in four different
missions, and had been in charge of Norwich and its dependent
parishes for the last seven years. He had therefore some experience as a superior, but none of lecturing, which did not

prevent him taking over the Moral classes. The retentive reader will remember him saying mass in the public house in Rhyl. After four years he was transferred to Preston, and then to Guiana where he became Bishop. There he had a reputation for 'straightforwardness, honesty, openness and manliness of character, and at the same time a kindliness and a geniality'. One hopes that the scholastics enjoyed the benefit of all those virtues when James was at St. Beuno's.

In 1855 Fr. William Cardwell (1855-57) was appointed Vice-Rector. In Jesuit parlance a vice-rector is someone appointed to do the job of Rector for an unspecified time. The amusing consequence has been that a vice-rector has sometimes had a longer term of office than most formally appointed rectors. Such was not the case with Fr. Cardwell, who relinquished the post in 1857. He had the advantage of knowing St. Beuno's as a student and as a lecturer. He had been one of the pioneers of '48. After his tertianship he taught Philosophy for a year, then came to St. Beuno's where he professed Dogma for four, but upon his appointment as Vice-Rector, with the fine flexibility of the period, took over Moral. He was only thirty-eight. As Superior he was found to be 'the soul of charity, no-one ever heard him say an unkind word', which makes it seem a pity that he only lasted two years. Ten years later he would return to teach Moral for four years.

His successor, both as Vice-Rector and Professor of Moral, George Lambert (1857-63) was straight from his tertianship and not quite thirty-six. At first his responsibilities were lessened by the withdrawal of all 'Longs' men to foreign theologates, which left him presiding over seventeen students and two lecturers. However, two years later a full staff and a proper complement of students of both courses were restored to him. One of his students was later to say 'we felt his presence not so much as a Superior, but as an example . . . because of his charity towards all, because of the readiness with which he lent an ear to every difficulty'.

Fr. Christopher Fitzsimon (1863-64), the next in line, was Irish by birth but educated at Stonyhurst. Maturer than his predecessors, being forty-eight, he was also more experienced. He had had charge of the Philosophers at the seminary, and for nine years was Socius to the Provincial, a kind of secretary and Man Friday, a position from which the working of the whole Province is perfectly visible. He became Superior of the Seminary in 1862, but was moved a year later to St. Beuno's. He stayed only a year before being made Novicemaster, his third appointment in three years. He was to be G.M.H.'s Novicemaster for a year.

Fr. Thomas Seed (1864-71) is of a wholly different variety. Born four years before John Etheridge, he came at the age of fifty-seven, which was comparatively venerable. Nor was he a promising ex-Tertian with intellectual possibilities. He had just relinquished the office of Provincial. With his accession St. Beuno's once more had a Rector. It would hardly have done to appoint an ex-Provincial merely Vice-Rector. Actually Thomas Seed is unlikely to have minded. When he left St. Beuno's in 1871, he asked to be given a class of young boys at Beaumont. Paradoxically, in his humility he had overestimated himself. He had lost the knack of controlling a class and had to leave. He returned to St. Beuno's as Spiritual Father, but died in 1874, and is buried just outside the Chapel door.

His successor, Alfred Weld (1871-73) was also an ex-Provincial, but somewhat younger, being forty-eight. Like Fr. Fitzsimon he was born in Ireland, but educated in England at Stonyhurst. He is something of a giant in his generation. He had begun as a promising astronomer, been made Superior of the Philosophers, then Novicemaster, before becoming Provincial at the age of forty-one. He spent only two years at St. Beuno's. In 1873 he was summoned to become the English Assistant to the General. In that post he performed some very delicate diplomatic work in Gibraltar and India and launched the Zambesi mission of which he was subsequently Superior. He died of Bright's Disease in South Africa. In his two years at St. Beuno's he certainly made his mark, planning the North Wing and the new rooms in Hamlets and Attica. The inhabitants of the latter additions may not have blessed his memory, finding their rooms cramped and draughty to the point of frigidity. Fr. Weld was vigorous and prompt to act; hence the extension. He was also somewhat over-sanguine, seeing things 'steeped in couleur de rose'; hence perhaps Hamlets and Attica. He is described as being during his brief stay at St. Beuno's 'on the best of terms with many of the principal families'. I wonder how many of St. Beuno's recent superiors could even tell you which the 'principal families' are.

James Jones (1873-76) was another Irishman, the third out of the first eight superiors, and had been educated not at Stonyhurst, but at Clongowes, the Irish equivalent. His history is anything but insular. He had started his noviceship on the continent, been transferred to England, studied theology in Sicily and Rome and worked in Guiana and Jamaica. He came to St. Beuno's to teach Moral, which he did for seven years before becoming Rector at the age of forty-five. As a lecturer his reputation was high, because he was judged to have 'experience, learning and breadth of view'. He was said to be a 'charming companion' at recreation. Was it at recreation that G.M.H. confessed to being so deeply moved at the death of the five German nuns, and heard Fr. Jones' comment that he wished someone would write a poem on the subject? Would that we had an account of the Rector's later reaction to the poem which his words had evoked!

Fr. Gallwey (1876-77), who succeeded when Fr. Jones became Provincial, was another Irishman educated at Stonyhurst. We met him in the class of '49. He had been Novicemaster after Fr. Fitzsimon. G.M.H.'s Rector during his ordination year was therefore the Novicemaster who had recommended him for vows, and the Provincial to whom he had 'manifested his conscience' during the previous three years. Fr. Gallwey remained only a year, during which much of his energy was spent trying to turn himself into a Moral theologian at the age of fifty-six.

In Thomas Rigby (1877-80) we have an undoubted Englishman from Preston, ex-Stonyhurst, of course, and nephew to Fr. Seed. We are also back to the younger man, as he was only thirty-five and had just finished his tertianship. He took over 'Shorts' for his first year, does not seem to have taught during his second, and during his third is described as teaching Scripture to 'Shorts'. This willingness to turn his hand to anything remains a characteristic. He went from St. Beuno's to teach Logic at Stonyhurst, worked in Liverpool for a year, in Guiana for fifteen, and then made up for being so long in one place by being in Wakefield, Malta, Bristol, London and Preston in the course of the next five.

Fr. Jones (1880-85), on laying down the office of Provincial, returned to St. Beuno's for a second term as Rector and Professor of Moral Theology. His period of office seems to have been quite pleasant but uneventful. He continued to teach Moral for another seven years until in 1892 he was summoned to the General

Congregation and chosen as English Assistant, but became ill and died. To a letter from St. Beuno's congratulating him on his appointment as Assistant he replied, 'I have loved St. Beuno's as I have never loved any other place, and I do not believe it will ever be supplanted in my affections . . . The same character and tone seem to be fixtures in the place, and I have not seen them elsewhere in the same form and colouring'. As he had first known St. Beuno's in 1855, and later spent twenty-one years as lecturer, Rector, Rector, lecturer, his tribute must carry weight.

Fr. Sylvester Hunter (1885-91) was a horse from a very different stable. Born in 1829 he was the son of a Unitarian minister, a pupil of St. Paul's, a scholar of Trinity College, Cambridge, and a first class mathematician. After Cambridge he took up the Law and wrote two textbooks which ran through several editions. He remained something of a polymath, keeping up his Greek and Latin and mathematics. He became a Catholic in 1857 and a novice in 1861. When he came to St. Beuno's he had been in charge of the Juniors' studies for ten years, but had never been a superior. As a man he was humble and conscientious, but 'singularly wanting in the gifts of the imagination'. As a result, 'he could not understand how anyone could know his duty and not do it, even in small things'. His careful, and to others exasperating, concern for legality led one of his fellow Jesuits to remark, 'Had Fr. Hunter lived in Our Lord's time he would have said, "Nos habemus legem, et secundum legem debet mori" ("We have a law, and by that law he ought to die")' (John 19.7). His three volume 'Outlines of Dogmatic Theology' are a better monument to his talents than the recollections of his rectorship.

With John Rickaby (1891-1901) we are back to the Stonyhurst product, but one with a difference, as John, the younger brother of 'Joe', was not a scion of the landed gentry, but the butler's second son. His lecturing methods, so stimulating to some, so frustrating to others, have already been described. The contrast between Fr. Hunter and Fr. Rickaby is summed up by their different attitudes to punishment when they were scholastics teaching boys. Fr. Hunter, the punctilious seeker after knowledge, went to the Prefect of Discipline and asked to receive the maximum number of 'ferulas', so that he would know exactly how severe a sanction he was wielding. Of John Rickaby a pupil later said, 'I cannot recall that he ever punished. He was always meditating how to interest us, and to soften the rigours of the class'. As John was Rector for the unusually long period of ten years, his rule must have given satisfaction to both superiors and subjects. Of the latter it is said that he enjoyed their 'affection and respect to a degree which he probably did not himself realise'.

John Clayton (1901-08), another Stonyhurst boy, was already sixty-one on appointment. He had been Rector of Mount St. Mary's immediately after his tertianship, and then Provincial. In 1893 he was appointed visitor to the New Orleans mission and then given powers of Provincial in that region till 1897, when he returned to England and became the first Rector of Wimbledon. He therefore came to St. Beuno's full of years and experience. He is described as 'marvellously tender in his judgement of others . . . and uncommonly good at holding his tongue'. The tribute which appeals to me most is, 'In his room, as you entered, down went his pen, and whether Priest, Scholastic or Brother, you were always welcome to his time'.

Charles Townsend (1908-15) was, like Sylvester Hunter, a convert, but an Oxford man, not a Cantabrigian. Ordained in the Anglican Church, he had been the Principal of the Oxford Mission in Calcutta before becoming a Catholic and a Jesuit. He entered the Belgian Province in the hopes of returning to India, but was claimed by the English Province and taught Classics to the Juniors. In 1906 he was appointed Professor of Scripture, and two years afterwards, at the age of fifty-four, Rector. He was incredibly learned, his pupils having given up the attempt to find out how many languages he could read when their total reached eleven. They respected even more the fact that 'he trusted everybody and they felt that they could not betray that trust'. Some of them were to cherish for the rest of their lives the memory of 'so self-effacingly kind and complete a gentleman and Jesuit'.

With the appointment of Alexander Keogh (1915-22) we are breaking new ground. Neither a Stonyhurst boy, nor a convert, he had been educated at a day school, St. Francis Xavier's, Liverpool and had been professionally prepared for his work by a biennium (official two-year course) in Church History at Innsbruck. He began to teach the subject in 1909, added Canon Law to his workload in 1912 and became Rector in 1915 when not quite forty-four. He was quick tempered and 'not very tolerant of divergent views', but his management was decidedly humane. He raised the wages of lay employees, put back the hour of rising from 5.00 a.m. to 5.30(!) and markedly improved the food. It is to be borne in mind that he was in charge of men in their thirties whose contemporaries, and even former pupils, were fighting, and all too often dying, in circumstances of nightmare not envisaged by G.M.H. when he wrote, 'Under her banner we fall for her honour'. As early as 1915 the scholastics were clamouring to be ordained and to be allowed to join their countrymen, even if it had to be in the uniform of a chaplain. At the end of his term of office he continued to teach Church History and Canon Law, and migrated with the theologate to Heythrop.

Henry Davis was, like his predecessor a Liverpool day boy. Unlike Fr. Keogh he had not been prepared for his teaching post by any specialist studies in his métier, which was Moral Theology. At the end of his tertianship he had been for a year Prefect of Juniors, then Prefect of Studies at Stonyhurst from 1903 to 1911. He was appointed to teach Moral in his forty-fifth year, and was nearly fifty-six when he became Rector. His story belongs at Heythrop rather than St. Beuno's. He was literally a legend in his own lifetime. His nickname, which was simply 'Father', sums up much of it. He was a dominant, more than lifesize figure, all-knowing and apparently without doubts. His four volumes of 'Moral Theology' were to be seen in practically every presbytery in the country. It is, of course, for his teaching and writing that he was so well known. His three years as Rector of St. Beuno's were not part of the legend.

A Jesuit rector in a large house will normally have four 'consultors', men of 'prudence and probity', with whom he discusses everything of importance, but without being bound by their opinions. Similarly, one stage up in the hierarchy, the Provincial will also have four consultors, with whom he should deliberate every month. House consultors not only offer their opinions to the Rector, they are required to write a report on the state of the house twice a year for the Provincial and once a year for the General. The Provincial consultors are also obliged to write to the General. When the Provincial sat down to discuss with his consultors the affairs of a place like St. Beuno's his information would have come from several sources, from his own annual visitation of the house, in which he had interviewed every member, from the reports of the Rector and the house consultors, and from anyone else who had seen fit to get in touch with him. He might also have been prodded into discussing St. Beuno's by the General, who received his own reports from the Provincial, the Provincial consultors, the Rector of St. Beuno's with the consultors thereof, and anyone else who had felt obliged to take the admittedly unusual step of writing directly and personally to the General, as any Jesuit is always free to do.

The notes of a Provincial consultation can be very revealing. They can also be quite misleading. They are revealing because they take us behind the scenes. They mislead because the Provincial and his counsellors do not meet to exchange congratulations on the successes of the Province. They are there to find solutions to its problems. The records of Provincial consultations are therefore instructive, but must be used with a sense of proportion. I wonder if the consultors themselves always kept theirs. House consultors often did not. The senior community at St. Beuno's, when it was a theologate, numbered ten, a small field in which to find four men who will always show themselves wise, observant, perceptive, objective and disinterested both in their judgement and the expression of it. One eccentric consultor of my younger days would, when the time came for him to write to the General, which he had to do in Latin, stump off to the room of some classicist and ask in thunderous tones, "Ow do you put into Latin, "The finances of this 'ouse are in the most incompetent 'ands"?' I doubt if his judgements were objective or his expression of them dispassionate.

Seen from the Provincial's equivalent of the cabinet table the solid time-resisting structure of St. Beuno's often looks surprisingly fragile. As early as 1849 the consultors were naturally worried about the emigré professors, who with the tide turning against the 'Revolution' would surely wing their way back to their own countries. In 1850 there is an interesting comment that the discipline is too severe. Perhaps the inexperienced John Etheridge was wisely making his initial mistakes on the side of strictness. By '55 there is anxiety about the expense of St. Beuno's. In 1857, ten years after its opening, the Provincial and his consultors seem to have despaired of its future. It was the year when they took the drastic step of sending 'Longs' abroad, and while 'Shorts' rattled round the half empty house, the Provincial was casting round for a buyer. If he had found one, 'Shorts' would probably have been returned to Stonyhurst, which would have plunged that site back into all the difficulties of the eighteen forties. The situation was further complicated by the wish to see the building remain in Catholic hands, and yet realise its cash value without delay. As Catholic bodies, flush with money and needing a neo-mediaeval building in North Wales were hard to come by, the 'Longs' were brought back and a staff scraped together to lecture them, while the Provincial went on wondering whether to pack them all back to Stonyhurst or to send them to the newly acquired property of Beaumont, Old Windsor. The instability of this period is reflected in the appointments of Vice-Rectors. Even that lesser appointment could present a problem, and in 1862 there was a good deal of headscratching until the Provincial's Socius, Fr. Fitzsimon, was thrust into the breach, only to be brought out again the following year, when they needed him for Novicemaster.

In 1865 one finds the comment that the staffing situation was deplorable, and in 1866 the General, who had presumably been kept informed, urged the removal of the scholastics to the neighbourhood of a large city, a suggestion made even before St. Beuno's was built, and one that was finally adopted only in 1970. Also in 1866 we find the Provincial and his prudent men deploring the expense of St. Beuno's and wishing that they could use the lecturers elsewhere. The matter drags on inconclusively, and in 1871 another rocket from the General on the standard of studies in the Province produces a further flurry of schemes. One is to combine philosophy and theology at St. Beuno's. Fr. Gallwey, at that time Novicemaster, wanted both faculties moved to London, while St. Beuno's could become another boys school. One consultor wanted the two faculties back at Stonyhurst. The Theologians could not be planned for in isolation. There were the Philosophers, the Juniors, the Lay Philosophers at Stonyhurst and the schools, which offered together a wealth of permutations. In '74 there is a suggestion that both Theologians and Philosophers move to Roehampton and that the boys at Mount St. Mary's move to St. Beuno's. The staff, it seems, were in favour of the two faculties being combined in an impressive academic institution, which could attract lay students, which would be more exciting, could offer the possibility of inviting people to disputations and give the students of one faculty the opportunity of attending lectures in the other. With Catholics still unable to attend the universities there was an outside chance of attracting some lay Catholics to an institution of higher learning, but I cannot imagine English Province Scholastics, their appetite for ecclesiastical learning more than satisfied by a daily overdose of Latin lectures, not to mention twice weekly disputations, eagerly attending academic occasions in the other faculty. Perhaps it was in response to this vision that Fr. Weld, inclined to see things 'in couleur rose', added so many rooms to a building whose future was so uncertain. In 1876, which is during G.M.H.'s period of residence, there is even an interesting suggestion that St. Beuno's might be purchased for a Carthusian monastery. This intriguing possibility, which was not unfavourably received by the consultors is the last one reads for some time concerning the moving of the theologate.

In 1876 Fr. Weld, now Assistant to the General, is urging the better formation of English professors, and the provision and the limitations of professors is the principal aspect of St. Beuno's to be discussed at provincial consultations throughout the eighties. We are told that the English lecturers find recreation trying rather than recreative. How the foreign professors found it we are not told. In '83 the departure of Fr. Wernz—who would one day be General of the Society—meant that there was no-one to teach Canon Law or Church History. As the gap was to remain for many a year, the question comes up frequently, and like other questions, remains unsolved. In 1883 we get the complaint that too many 'dead' questions are discussed at too great a length in lectures, and that the Scripture Professor, the long-serving Fr. Perini, gives a quite unpractical course. In '85 instructions come from the Vicar General that they should find a new Scripture teacher, and the veteran Perini handed over to G.M.H.'s contemporary, Sydney Smith. In '86 there is a complaint that the theses of one professor contradict those of another. The consultors, I am glad to say, gave their opinion that the subject under discussion admitted of a plurality of views.

During the eighties there are also complaints from the house consultors of unpunctual rising, i.e. later than 5.00 a.m.! They also report that the rule of speaking Latin is inadequately observed and that recreation is often replaced by practices for ceremonies. One hopes that the last complaint was made out of solicitude for the scholastics' recreation period and not sheer fussiness. It is also reported several times that the laybrothers are drinking too much beer. One is not to imagine the brothers throwing raucous beer parties. Beer was served at dinner, and the brothers at 'second table' probably finished off the surplus as well as disposing of their own ration, to the scandal of some sourpuss of a consultor. As the complaint goes on, we can presume that no action was taken and that, at least for some years, the brothers continued to enjoy their extra glass.

At the end of the eighties there are complaints that the Rector—Sylvester Hunter, the lawyer—is too harsh. If so, his legalism did not extend to the house's drinking habits, as the brothers' extra drink remains uncurtailed and the scholastics are sometimes taking four glasses of wine on feast days. And too much tobacco and snuff is being consumed! After the accession of the liberal John Rickaby, there are several allegations of lack of discipline, of too much novel reading, of 'Protestant Books' being read, of the new extravagant practice of sending Christmas cards, of excessive piano playing, of too much time being devoted to the preparation of plays and operettas, at which the actors sometimes wear dresses, of young priests (minimum age thirty-four!) being allowed too many visits to outsiders. The Province consultors do not seem to have been greatly perturbed by these strictures. They rightly gave more thought to the suggestion that the Theologians should be transferred to Wimbledon. The new location would be more stimulating to both teachers and students; outsiders could be attracted to lectures; the community could be a good influence in the capital and bishops might be invited to formal disputations. The counter-argument was the usual one of the young men's need of exercise and clean air. In '98 there was a suggestion that the Theologians should move to Roehampton and the novitiate be transferred to St. Beuno's. Against that proposal someone objected that to train novices at St. Beuno's would be to bring them up like monks. Did he consider that it was having that effect on the Province's priests?

As Fr. Rickaby's long Rectorship drew to a close there was much trouble finding his successor. The short list of three sent up to the General, who made the final selection, was turned down in toto. A second list seems to have gone the same way. The post eventually went to John Clayton, who had been a Provincial, and had had years of experience as a Rector. He had even managed the affairs of the Jesuits of Louisiana. The arrival of the twentieth century does not bring any significant change in the preoccupations of house consultors' reports. There is the usual arraignment of venial shortcomings; unpunctual rising, breaches of silence and too much novel reading. Even the General was persuaded by some consultor or consultors in 1903 that the students over-indulged in light literature. A new complaint is that too much time is spent on the golf course, although it is conceded that the game has contributed to the health of the student body. In 1912 the Provincial and his consultors ruled that the scholastics might walk in the grounds at evening recreation, even in the winter, provided that they kept to the paths, a decision which, no doubt, contributed greatly to the evangelisation of Britain in subsequent years!

The vastly experienced Fr. Clayton seems to have been somewhat too masterful. Consultors say that he monopolises power, that he makes large purchases without consultation, that the Minister has too little scope. There are complaints of continuing discomfort. In '05 it is said that there have been no baths for months. However, the Province consultors decide that, although he is no theologian and somewhat unconstitutional in his ways, he is generally popular in the house, in which there exists a general spirit of study . . . And so it goes on. No Rector is going to be wholly wise; no scholastic community impeccable, at least not for a year at a time.

One further item of house discipline is, I think, worth brief notice. In 1916 the Provincial and his consultors had to deal with a complaint about the lifting of 'enclosure', i.e. the admission to the house of women guests on ordination day. The same issue had been raised in 1888. On both occasions the consultors with the Provincial decided that the custom was to be upheld, and the ladies welcomed. Two aspects of the matter interest me; first, that a sweeping, but not irrational, mediaeval regulation should have developed for some people into such a highly charged irrefrangible tabu; secondly, the date of the complaint, 1916. They were in the middle of The Great War. The industrial skills and the organisational progress which had been going to make Europe wealthy, healthy and educated, were instead helping the men of Europe to kill and maim one another on a scale previously unimaginable. The Theologians to their credit were impatient to be alongside their brothers and friends and ex-pupils. Thirty-three priests of the

Province were already acting as chaplains. And one mind at St. Beuno's was exercised over the legitimacy of a Provincial exemption from 'enclosure' which admitted mothers, sisters and aunts to the house for a part of one day in the year.

St Beuno on the left with St Beuno's on his arm.
He has the original building which ended with the tower

XI

Queen's move: Tertians take the tower

The dawn of the twentieth century did not dissipate the growing gloom over St. Beuno's academic condition. Rather it highlighted the fact that the Province was again dependent on lecturers from the continent, that its physical isolation was paralleled by the scholastic remoteness of its courses from the theological issues of the day. In 1900 consultors complain that Fr. Tepe is not up to date and rouses no enthusiasm. In 1901 it is said that the Moral Professor (Fr. Slater) the canonist turned moralist, lacks concrete experience. In 1902 a commission was set up to investigate the higher studies of the Province. The commission included Fr. Browne, Rector of Stonyhurst, Fr. Maher of the Philosophy staff and John Gerard of The Month. That the situation was unsatisfactory was agreed on all sides. Some of the staff blame the scholastics for lack of interest, even for a certain resistance, and complain of an inadequate grasp of Latin and in some students a generally defective education. Fr. Jaggar, the Prefect of Studies at St. Beuno's, wrote a report which is quite at variance with the picture one gets of him as a rhetorician lacking incisiveness. He urged that divergent Scholastic theories should receive less attention, that the Professors should be better acquainted with the work of rationalists and able to expound them to the students, that Higher Biblical criticism should be studied, and that more attention should be given to the historical aspect of Theology. Church history should pay more attention in a British context to the Papacy, Holy orders etc. There should be a separate teacher of Canon Law, and there was need of men competent in Oriental languages and trained in Ecclesiastical History. The isolation of St. Beuno's was deplorable. Professors can only keep in touch through magazines and reviews. The house is insufficiently connected with the working Province and would benefit greatly if it were sited where outsiders might come to lectures and disputations.

The commission's findings were favourable to the students, pointing out that English scholastics sent to Ireland were not found defective in either attitude or intellectual equipment. They declared that an average age of thirty-one among first year students was an initial handicap, that professors from abroad were unlikely to gear their courses to the English intellectual situation, that the staff in general were out of contact with live theological issues and that current theological literature was not available to the students. Their principal conclusion was that the theologate should be moved to a place more in contact with the life of the times. The Provincial, Fr. Colley, writing to the General in the following year, defended the scholastics and criticised the studies as lacking in a sense of the contemporary.

In 1907 the General, Fr. Wernz, who had once lectured for a year at St. Beuno's, suggested that Theology and Philosophy should be combined in one Collegium Maximum near London or a large city. The consultors accepted the principle. Philosophy, one of them opined, had become an annex of Stonyhurst, while Theology was 'lost in the Welsh hills'. A Collegium Maximum would enliven the staff with its cross fertilisation of faculties, especially in the setting of London or some other large city. The General's suggestion revived for some the dream of a house of studies which would attract diocesan students to its benches and perhaps an interested public. Fr. Joseph Rickaby, when consulted, proffered a vision all his own of a collegium at Stonor Park, near Henley, redolent with the heroic tradition of Fr. Parsons' printing press and in contact with Oxford. There were counter-arguments old and new. The importance of fresh air and exercise was invoked yet again. The subtraction of the Philosophers would, in the opinion of one consultor, reduce the prestige of Stonyhurst to the loss of the Province. Fr. Purbrick, an Oxford convert who had been Provincial both in England and the U.S.A., proposed the building of a Catholic University on the Stonyhurst site. Fr. Joseph Browne opposed the notion of a Collegium Maximum on the grounds that the community would be too large for any one Rector, and that the members would lack real pastoral care and the training of the Theologians as priests suffer in consequence. Some graduates of the Heythrop Collegium Maximum may think he had a point.

Eventually the Provincial, Fr. Sykes, replied to the General, saying that the scheme was not immediately practicable because of the huge financial outlay it would involve. He was succeeded in

1910 by Fr. Browne, whose distaste for the plan may partly explain why the Theologians lingered at St. Beuno's in spite of the prodding of Fr. General and the criticisms of so many eminent members of the Province. The tide of history did not slacken, but reached new heights during the post-war years, when the Province, like some Canute sodden to the waist and scrambling to dry ground, purchased Heythrop Hall, a mansion originally reared by the only Duke of Shrewsbury. To this Oxfordshire pile the Province added two large wings, one where Theology, the Queen of the Sciences, might hold her court and the other in which Philosophy, the handmaid, could discharge her propaedeutic task. Thither in the late summer of 1926 came the disciples of both, and the new Collegium Maximum was inaugurated. A few months later a philosopher was to write a blithe description of the move concluding, 'The life of St. Mary's Hall has been preserved intact and transplanted to Oxfordshire, and all the customs and traditions of the old regime have as far as possible been retained'. Oh dear! Had Canute simply moved his chair further up the beach?

With a two mile drive between Heythrop and the main road, and Oxford some thirteen miles beyond the junction, the Collegium Maximum could hardly be described as 'near a large town'. It was certainly better equipped than St. Beuno's. At St. Beuno's a full complement of lecturers meant six men, and for years on end they had made do with five. I during my Theology course was taught by twelve different lecturers, each well qualified in his subject, and not one of them a foreigner! In front of the house lay broad, flat playing fields and there was an outdoor swimming pool, which was also a reservoir in case of fire, the formula which had been planned at St. Beuno's and abandoned unfinished. Yet for all our twelve home-grown Professors and the lovely cricket flat, Heythrop, as I knew it, remained open to some of the criticism levelled at St. Beuno's fifty years before. If the train journey from Charlbury to London was shorter than that from Rhyl, we were still being brought up in a distant rural setting, where, I used to think, it would seem quite natural to go to sleep for half the year. More to the point, I left Philosophy with an undeservedly high mark in 1946 having never heard the names of Ayer or Wittgenstein. I left Theology in 1956 with quite modest results, but sharing with my more successful contemporaries a complete ignorance of the work of Karl Barth and a quite hazy

notion as to what was meant by Form Criticism. These facts I
record not out of senile resentment, but in extenuation of St.
Beuno's.

St. Beuno's was, I suspect, the better house in one respect. The
Theologians lived in St. Beuno's with a handful of lecturers and
officials and a small group of brothers, knowing that the house
was for them. Heythrop in Oxfordshire belonged to nobody. It
contained the Theologians, the Philosophers, a senior community
which in 1926 numbered twenty-two, with seventeen brothers. The
total came to 191 bodies, which is larger than the entire province
in 1848 (total 182), though smaller than the German College at
Valkenburg, which in 1919 could boast of 317 Jesuits. Perhaps the
prescient Fr. Browne knew something about Valkenburg.

As the Theologate evacuates St. Beuno's let us take one last look
at it. One aspect of its period in North Wales may need a little
more emphasis, namely the fact that the Theologians were so
much part of the local scene. In the early days they were invited
to those otter hunts. Fr. Weld had been on good terms with 'the
principal families'. In 1863 a barrel of tar was hoisted to the top of
the Rock and a 'monster bonfire' lit on the slope beneath to
celebrate the wedding of the Prince of Wales. In 1887 for the
Golden Jubilee of the Queen the students helped to organise
village sports and to serve a 'subtantial dinner' to 700 villagers, the
cost of which was largely borne by the College. At night there
were fireworks and illuminations. Ten years later, for the Diamond
Jubilee, there was another dinner with fireworks and illuminations.
For the coronation of George V the formula was repeated, but the
celebrations were somewhat marred by the fact that the Minister,
Fr. Dobson, when making his own fireworks, set off an explosion
and lost his left hand. Legend had it in my young days that,
when visited in hospital, he was sitting up teaching himself to roll
cigarettes with only one hand. In 1911 the Rector and Fr. Jaggar
were invited to the Installation of the Prince of Wales. St. Beuno's
at that time 'belonged'.

The Great War affected the Theologians keenly. Perhaps there
was an extra dimension to their emotional involvement because
the Province was receiving accounts from Belgian Jesuits of the
course of the German invasion, while the French Jesuits, who
were being called to the colours, had mostly been trained in their
houses of exile at Mold, Hastings and Jersey. A score of the

Theologians were to go from St. Beuno's to the services with little time between. One such was Walter Montague, who was ordained on April 25th, 1918, and in France by May 21st. He died of wounds on October 31st. His name leads the list of Tremeirchion's war dead on the memorial outside the village church. Eighty members of the Province served as chaplains, five dying on active service. The Theologians tried to get on with their studies, helped on the farm and even collected sphagnum moss for medical purposes. Fr. Keogh, as we saw, moved the rising hour to 5.30, the only structural change, it seems, in the life of St. Beuno's which can be attributed to the First World War.

In 1925 ten members of the English Province began their Theology at St. Beuno's, the last members of the Province to do so. They make an interesting, though not exciting contrast with the men of '49. Gone are the days when the Province consisted only of Stonyhurst boys and converts. Stonyhurst, Glasgow, Beaumont, Leeds and Preston are all represented in 1925, but the largest single group of old boys are the three from Mount St. Mary's nr Chesterfield. A quite different flavour is added by the presence of Samuel Hornby, who had left Burnley Secondary School at the age of fifteen, and joined the Society after the war. The social make-up of the Province had changed. The careers of the ten are also typical of the period. Two went to Africa; one to Guiana. Only two spent their lives in the parishes. Fr. Basil Fitzgibbon became a meticulous scholar of Elizabethan and Early Stuart history, and four went teaching, one of them, Fr. Wilkin, later leaving the classroom to become a well-loved University chaplain.

Of all the English Jesuits who between 1848 and 1925 had started their Theology course at St. Beuno's, the most widely known in his own day was Bernard Vaughan, who arrived in the year that G.M.H. left, 1877. His preaching made him a national figure, attracting even Edward, Prince of Wales, to his sermons and earning him laudatory obituaries in all the principal newspapers of England. Herbert Thurston, who began his Theology in '87, has some claim to being the most prolific of St. Beuno's alumni. He was a highly respected historian who published a total of 727 books and articles, which figure does not include book reviews. Perhaps the most brilliant of St. Beuno's products was George Tyrrell, who arrived a year after Fr.

Thurston, with whom he maintained a close friendship till death. Fr. Tyrrell was subtle, mentally energetic, highly imaginative, and as a writer, both incisive and moving. He could be presented as an apostate, an extreme Modernist, and as moving towards mere pantheism. He could also be put forward as an outstandingly perspicacious and courageous Catholic condemned and excluded because he was almost a century ahead of his contemporaries. It is to the credit of the Province that it attracted a man of his stature, trained him, held him as long as it did, and gave him several warm, enduring friendships. It would have been even more to the credit of the Society if his letter to the General of 1904 had been humbly reflected upon by the Society's leadership. No stricture by George Tyrrell was likely to be utterly baseless.

Alban Goodier came to St. Beuno's to start Theology in 1900. He later became Archbishop of Bombay, and, retiring in 1925 wrote 'The Public Life Of Our Lord' and 'The Passion and Death Of Our Lord', works which were to be found on almost every Catholic bookshelf. These volumes and some of his other writings deeply moved at least two generations of the devout. Charles Plater ('07) is still remembered for his consuming interest in social and economic problems and his over-strenuous efforts to disseminate Catholic social teaching. He died at only forty-five. Cyril Martindale ('08) was a gifted and promising scholar who became far more interested in reaching out to the mass of his fellow countrymen. His disarming, mellifluous voice enabled him to speak to them 'on the wireless'; his intellectual energy and verbal felicity ensured a prodigious flow of books and pamphlets. Martin D'Arcy ('21) remained in the academic world, commissioned the architect Lutyens to plan a new Campion Hall in Oxford, and filled the completed building with works of art. He had the intimate friendship of artists, writers and academics of the first rank. As Master of Campion Hall forty years after him, I would still meet Oxford figures who would remember with admiration and affection his kindness to them when they were undergraduates. James Brodrick ('22) was in his day as well represented in Catholic libraries as anyone, earning his place there with his carefully researched saints' lives, some of which read as vividly as a good novel. Among all the graduates of St. Beuno's my own moral pin-up, as I have already admitted, is Thomas Roberts ('23), who resigned the Archbishopric of Bombay so that India's most important see might be filled by an Indian. After this impressive act of kenosis he continued to show a complete lack of interest in place, pomp or approval. After careful reflection he said quite unpretentiously, indeed almost boringly, what he thought, cheerfully risking the disapproval of authority.

To this history of the St. Beuno's Theologate I must add a tailpiece. Of Heythrop in Oxfordshire I stated that in the nineteen fifties our course still suffered from the fault so often urged against St. Beuno's, that it lagged behind the times, hardly acknowledging modern theologians and contemporary issues. This defect seemed to me to have been remedied when I used to visit Heythrop in the sixties. In 1970 Heythrop College moved to Cavendish Square in the middle of London. In 1971 the College was granted a Royal Charter, establishing it as one of the Schools and Institutes of the Federal University of London. Jesuit scholastics are only a fraction of the student body which is predominantly lay, and the teaching is shared by members of other congregations, members of other denominations and lay people. In one strenuous, courageous, imaginative burst, admittedly lasting some years, the professional studies of the English Province caught up with the times.

With the departure of the Theologians St. Beuno's stood for a year not empty, but two thirds unoccupied. It housed nine priests, three of them listed as 'cur. val.' or invalids. One of them was John Rickaby, the stimulating, but to some tantalising, lecturer. Also in the house was his elder brother 'Joe', the last survivor of G.M.H.'s year. He is listed as 'scriptor' i.e. occupied in writing. Of the nine remaining laybrothers four are entered as 'cur. val.' The poor infirmarian must have had a busy time. He had the energy, being only twenty-four. He was already amassing the experience which led the Heythrop doctor to remark to me in 1944, 'In some ways Brother Melling is as good as a doctor'.

If the old men and perhaps the younger brothers found the empty tables in the dining room and the unoccupied benches in the Chapel depressing, and yearned a little for the days of the young—comparatively young—Theologians, their longings were to be partly assuaged by the arrival of the Tertians in the autumn of 1928. I say 'partly' because the Tertians were a little older than the oldest Theologians, and the way of life of the Tertians more circumscribed and much more subdued in tone. The word 'Tertian' used for the Jesuit in his last year of formation comes from the phrase 'the Third Year of Probation'. It is a 'third' year in that it is linked to some extent in purpose, and to quite an extent in method with the noviceship, which lasts two years. Hopkins underwent his tertianship at Roehampton and explained its nature and purpose to Canon Dixon: 'This Tertianship or Third Year of Probation . . . is not really a noviceship at all in the sense of a time during which a candidate or probationer makes trial of our life and is free to withdraw. At the end of the noviceship proper we take vows which are perpetually binding and renew them every six months (not for every six months but for life) till we are professed . . . It is in preparation for these last vows that we make the tertianship; which is called a schola affectus and is meant to enable us to recover that fervour which may have cooled through application to study and contact with the world. Its exercises are however nearly the same as those of the first noviceship'. The poet of sprung rhythm, arcane vocabulary and verbal fabrication was, as we see here, quite capable of simple, lucid, factual explanation and I shall not presume to add to his statement.

The order of the day observed by the Tertians of 1927 at St. Beuno's shows something of the means by which the purpose of the Tertianship was sought.

5.30	Rise. Meditation
7.00 and 7.30	Masses
8.00	Breakfast
9.45	Manual work
10.20	By heart
11.30	Lecture
12.15	Vespers and Compline
12.45	Examination of Conscience
1.00	Dinner. Recreation
2.30	Free time
3.20	Reading of A Kempis and a saint's biography
4.00	Matins and Lauds
4.45	Coffee
5.15	Conference
5.45	Visit to Chapel
6.00	Institute Studies
6.30	Spiritual Reading

6.55	Meditation
7.30	Supper
8.30	Recreation
9.00	Litanies. Prepare morning Meditation
	Examination of Conscience
10.00	Lights out

As a Tertian in 1955-56 I followed, or was supposed to, substantially the same programme. I do not remember there being a time for reading A Kempis' 'Imitation Of Christ' and hagiography, and I think that we had rather longer for 'Institute Studies'.

There were masses at both 7.00 and 7.30 because there were in 1927 ten priests in the senior community besides thirty-three tertians, who, of course, had been ordained after their third years of theology. There were therefore forty-three masses to be accommodated, the number rising in 1932-33 to fifty-four! Altars were erected wherever they could be decently fitted in, and were used twice and perhaps three times each morning. As one did not say mass alone, but needed a server, the Tertians doubled up, i.e. one said mass while the other served, and then they reversed roles. On Christmas night and All Souls Day each priest said three masses, so one was involved in six brisk masses ere break of day. This battery hen arrangement always seemed to me quite irreverent, and I used to pine for the Eastern practice of concelebration. My wish was fulfilled in the following decade and when I stayed at St. Beuno's in 1969 I was happy to join the Tertians in a concelebrated mass.

Manual work was one of the similarities with the noviceship. We swept corridors, laid the dining room table, split logs. We also served in the refectory and washed up. As during the summer one had presided at solemn sung masses garbed in rich velvet and fine linen and preached to large congregations, it was salutary to find oneself wielding dust-pan and brush on the staircase, and somehow breathing in more of the dust than ever seemed to find its way into the dust-pan. 'By heart' was a venerable tradition. The early Jesuits believed very firmly in cultivating a word-perfect memory, a valuable facility when the printing press was still comparatively cumbersome and expensive, and not even the age of the tape recorder has made an accurate memory wholly redundant. Our novicemaster set us a battery of classical prayers to learn, which, he said, would stand us in good stead when we were old and ill and reading with difficulty. My eye-sight has outlasted my memory and the prayers are now forgotten except for the 'Adoro Te'. I should have recited them regularly. As a Junior, after the noviceship, I learned some Shakespeare sonnets and tried to master 'Lycidas'. I did not quite succeed, but I did come to realise how for Milton every consonant counts. Don't ask me what I tried to learn during the Tertianship. I didn't.

The 11.30 lecture for most of the year was on the 'Institute' and it was that which was meant to be the principal subject of our evening studies. The aims of the Society, its structure, its practices, its system of training, the duties and rights of its officials etc. have over four centuries generated a good deal of legislation. This has been digested into a handbook of less than 900 pages, 'The Constitutions and Epitome Of The Institute Of The Society Of Jesus'. This work we were expected to know our way around. The Instructor expounded it, and commented on it, and we were examined in it before the end of the year. Towards the end of the year, the 'Institute' safely aside, the Instructor lectured on ascetical theology, carefully getting the subject up for the purpose. We also received visits from members of the Province engaged in less traditional ministries such as the social apostolate and marriage guidance.

The evening conferences were given by the Tertians themselves. One of them every week was devoted to a 'case of conscience' i.e. an exercise in Moral Theology. Such was the primacy of that subject; nobody was worrying whether our grip on Dogma might be slipping. Lectures and conferences were suspended while we prepared for Lent, not for its austerities, but for the parish missions and other work to which we were sent out. Towards the end of the year we prepared eight-day retreats to be given in the summer. As in the 'preached' retreats of those days there were four talks a day to be given, there were thirty-two talks to be made ready. I knew that I was going to spend the summer in a retreat house where there were only weekend retreats, and so dispensed myself from this labour. I don't think that I was lazy; I just did not like preparing material for a purely imaginary audience. While I was at the retreat house, the Tertian Instructor was taken ill and unable to give the eight-day retreat at a convent close by, and I was called upon to fill in. My thirty-two talks had to be composed, each just before it was delivered.

On Sunday and Tuesday afternoons the Tertians went for walks or played volley-ball. Thursday was free of lectures or study of any kind and we tramped the countryside, weather permitting. I ought to make it clear that the various sections of office dotted around the daily programme were not being chanted in chapel, but recited privately. I always took it that the set times were optional. I did not think highly of saying compline just after midday. Come to think of it, I do not seem to have been an altogether co-operative Tertian.

As the Tertians took over St. Beuno's in 1927 and ceded it temporarily to the Novices in 1939, I am in the cart-before-the-horse situation of describing the last year of formation before the first two. My explanation of the Tertian's day and week will not, therefore, have brought out the accuracy of G.M.H.'s statement that its exercises are 'nearly the same as those of the noviceship'. Those exercises are the 'Long Retreat', the study of the Constitutions, manual work and an enhanced programme of prayer. The 'Thirty Days', or the full Spiritual Exercises were made both in the Noviceship and the Tertianship, the Tertianship version being somewhat more rigorous with midnight meditations and briefer breaks. As novices we had the essentials of the Jesuit Constitutions and the staple practices of the Society carefully explained. As tertians we tackled the more elaborate and intricate 'Epitome'. Both groups did manual work, the novices spending far more time in the gardens, their young bodies requiring rather more fresh air and exercise, their youthful spirits needing more relief from the rather intense and somewhat claustrophobic atmosphere within the house. Both novices and tertians added to the ordinary round of spiritual duties an evening meditation.

Also common to both periods of training, though hardly to be called an 'exercise', was the policy of effecting, or rather trying to bring about, a single-minded focus on the spiritual by a policy of more than monastic seclusion, not only socially but intellectually. 'They will not read newspapers, periodicals etc. nor any books but spiritual books'. For the most part we spoke to nobody outside our immediate group, met nobody, visited nobody. And from this wholesale pruning the Society anticipated a rich interior fruitfulness in us all.

XII

The finishing school and the kindergarten

Of his tertianship at Roehampton G.M.H. wrote cheerfully enough, 'in eremo sumus' (we are in the desert). I suspect that with the coming of the Tertians St. Beuno's began to be estranged from its North Wales setting. Tertians certainly did not join the gentry in their field sports or go excavating tumuli on their land. Spending less than a year in Wales, they were not tempted to learn the Welsh language so that they might converse for apostolic purposes with people to' whom they were not allowed to talk. Did their austerely 'spiritual' library contain a Welsh grammar or a Welsh dictionary? I never saw one in my own day. This isolation from the neighbourhood would have been reinforced by the withdrawal, for reasons which had nothing to do with the Tertians, of the Jesuits from the local parishes. From 1929 to 1933 the Society transferred to their respective dioceses in different parts of Britain fifteen parochial missions, of which several were connected with St. Beuno's. Holywell was handed over in 1930, ending almost three and a half centuries of Jesuit service. Rhyl and St. Asaph went in 1931, Denbigh in 1932 and St. Beuno's ceased to send a priest to Ruthin in 1933.

Also with the Theologians departed a certain exuberance. Tertians did not produce operettas, stage debates on public affairs or march all the way to Barmouth. They were birds of passage, here only from October to July, birds of sober plumage and little song. A diet of the 'Epitome', extra meditation and unrelievedly 'spiritual' reading without news or contacts generated little in the way of hilarity. G.M.H. had quite liked it. 'My mind is here more at peace than it has ever been and I would gladly live all my life, if it were so to be in as great or a greater seclusion from the world and be busied only with God'. Most English Jesuits were far less contemplative by nature. For them such seclusion was something to be endured, by some placidly, by others more restively.

For me my tertianship, made 1955-56, was the least satisfactory part of my training, and I suspect that it was so for many others.

This is no severe indictment. After all, some section of that long, variegated process of formation had to be less effective than the others. I fully realised my need of a sabbatical in the 'schola affectus'. After two years as an overworked teaching scholastic, three as an anxious undergraduate and four of Theology, I certainly needed to irrigate my soul with prayer, to dig over the soil of my personal commitment and fertilise it with painstaking reflection assisted by good reading. Two factors worked adversely. First, our training had, through no-one's fault and because of the numbers involved, become something of a factory process. Numbers, I say again, lest I sound censorious, hardly permitted anything else, and the industrialisation of European life had made such handling, even of human beings, seem quite normal. Such an approach was impoverishing in the academic part of our training; in the 'schola affectus' it was blighting. Secondly, although G.M.H. throve in it, I found the return to noviceship conditions stultifying. I had come to the noviceship straight from school at the age of seventeen. I entered the tertianship at thirty-three, a very different being. Not only had I studied Philosophy, Theology and History and read quite widely in literature, I had been a schoolmaster in a grammar school and for eighteen months a weekend chaplain on a U.S.A.F. base: I had been a priest for two years and heard confessions and preached in almost a score of churches. My experience as a teacher and a priest had taught me the need of a deep, robust spirituality which would cope with bustle, anxiety and overwork. The hothouse conditions of a return to noviceship restrictions and methods seemed to me the last place to grow such a plant.

I doubt whether at the time I could have articulated the situation in quite that way, but the same thoughts were stirring and creating something of a malaise, which, I think, was commonly shared. The atmosphere was therefore normally one of resignation rather than of happy expectation. For most people it was not an unhappy time. We were free for a year from the many lectures and frequent exams of Heythrop; the members of the English Province knew one another well and the admixture of people from abroad added interest; almost everyone had learned over the years to live in community inoffensively. To some extroverts the life was galling; I have come across some people who, like Hopkins, claim to have been happy and benefited; most of us accepted it. The Tertianship did not, to use an expression of one of my early Rectors, 'add much to the gaiety of nations' . . . or of St. Beuno's.

The first group of Tertian Instructors were certainly men of calibre. Fr. James Bridge (1927-31) had taught General Metaphysics to the Philosophers, been Prefect of Studies at Liverpool and then Rector and Parish Priest, also at Liverpool, and filled the office of Tertian Instructor in Ireland for seven years before coming to St. Beuno's. He had secured a First at Oxford, proved a lucid, if uninspiring lecturer, was a competent Prefect of Studies and a zealous parish priest. Unfortunately, 'he lacked one element, and that an essential one—imagination. He took too objective a view of his responsibility, endeavouring to fit all shapes and sizes into the mould of the Rule as he interpreted it'. His successor, Joseph Bolland (1931-34) was even more of an intellectual and had a more distinguished career. He had shone at Oxford, taught three out of the six main subjects to the Philosophers and then specialised in the History of Philosophy. He was only Instructor for three years before being summoned to the office of Provincial. Retiring from the office, he informed his successor that he was tired of improving his mind, and became a curate at Leigh. There he passed six happy years, a success it seems with every group in the parish, especially the Polish exiles, whose language he dutifully studied. He spent the last ten years of life in Rome as English Assistant, dying as a result of a street accident. Leonard Geddes (1934-38) had taught Apologetics at St. Beuno's before the migration, been Superior of the Philosophers while professing General Metaphysics and had a second spell of teaching Apologetics. He then changed faculties once more, teaching another part of the Philosophy syllabus. It is said that in none of the subjects which he taught did he show 'any vital interest'. Like Fr. Bridge he notoriously lacked imagination and was 'somewhat legalist in his tackling of human problems . . . he was somewhat at a loss with the individual who did not quite fit in or who betrayed anything like eccentricity'.

All three Instructors were men of learning and experience. The 'Long Retreat' of thirty days, which in those years required five addresses a day, they would have given conscientiously and competently, Fr. Bolland achieving a greater depth than the other two. As tutors in the 'schola affectus' they were less qualified. The 'affectus' must be an individual, personal affair, even unique to the individual. One can preach attitudes to a group, but the growth of the corresponding dispositions must vary in each person. The Tertian is less in need of being told what his attitudes should be than of guidance in examining his past responses to the challenge of the 'Exercises' and seeing his way forward. Yet it was precisely in the area of the individual that the signally unimaginative Fr. Bridge and Fr. Geddes were at their weakest, while the highly cerebral Fr. Bolland was 'an incurable dialectician', a grave weakness in a counsellor.

Fr. Bridge had an average of thirty-five tertians a year, Fr. Bolland thirty-seven, Fr. Geddes thirty-eight, although the actual record goes to Fr. Bolland, who in two consecutive years had forty-two charges. Quite often more than a score of the Tertians were from abroad, drawn from eight or nine different provinces. A fat chance any Instructor had of offering such an unwieldy, variegated mass anything like personal guidance at any depth! I suspect that in an age of mass production, of universal education, of, in many countries, general military conscription the concept of patient, delicate, personal guidance passed into eclipse.

One detail: it is a curious fact that all three of those first St. Beuno's Instructors had been pupils at Mount St. Mary's, Fr. Lythgoe's first educational venture outside Stonyhurst. The Instructor was not the Rector of the house. The Rector was a benign, constitutional monarch keeping, as far as the Tertians were concerned, discreetly to the background. He kept a paternal eye on the senior community with its three or four retired priests and on the dozen laybrothers whose invaluable lives not only kept the domestic machine functioning, but, as each year's crop of Tertians came and went without encountering their predecessors or their successors, contributed a much needed element of continuity. Fr. Francis Holme presided over the house during the tenantless year of 1926-27 with the title of Superior. Fr. Joseph Martin became Rector in 1927 and was succeeded in 1931 by Fr. Frederick Parry, who had a thoroughly deserved reputation, not only as an administrator, but as a Superior 'kind and generous beyond words'. In February 1939, at the age of seventy-four, he handed over to Fr. Thomas Eastham, who was to see seven months later Europe at war and St. Beuno's swarming with more than half a hundred novices, the seventeen-year-old Paul Edwards among them.

Before we leave the pre-war Tertianship and turn to the evacuee
novices I must offer the substance of my first interview in
preparation for this work. It was with a survivor of the 1938-39
Tertianship. In that year Fr. Geddes withdrew after the Long
Retreat, and the rest of the time passed under the direction of Fr.
Henry Keane, who had preceded Fr. Bolland in the office of
Provincial. Fr. Keane's lectures were, in the opinion of my inform-
ant, fascinating. One phrase had lingered: 'You must have the
motivation and not the machinery'. The Tertians had accepted the
regulations contentedly and the year had been a decidedly happy
one. This experience chimes with that of G.M.H. almost sixty
years before, but not with mine seventeen years later. Nor is it the
general impression I received from the men I went to work among
in 1956. Examining the obituary accounts of the first three Instructors I was struck by the small amount of space given to their work
in that office, compared with the detailed descriptions of them in
other roles. I risk the conclusion that public opinion in the English
Province did not consider the Tertianship to be that significant.

'In general, it would be true to say that the outbreak of war
took the Province at unawares'. I am still taken aback re-reading
that comment of Fr. Mangan who, having become Provincial on
August 29th, 1939, was certainly in a position to know. After the
invasion of Czechoslovakia, the issue of gas masks and the call-up
of the twenty year old men even a lad of sixteen knew that war
was on its way. Where was the legendary Jesuit astuteness? Or
had the highly intelligent, sceptical Fr. Bolland (Provincial 1934-39)
decided that the shape and effects of the war were quite unpredictable, and planning for it a waste of time? He had promised the
authorities that in the event of war the Province would provide
twelve priests as chaplains. By 1945 it had sent eighty-six, so
perhaps he was right. One of Fr. Mangan's first steps was to
cancel the Tertianship and send the novices to St. Beuno's. The '39
intake made its way to North Wales on September 28th joining the
Second Year already in possession. There were then eighty Jesuit
bodies under the roof, the largest number St Beuno's had seen.
We fitted easily enough, because there were two novices to a
room, except in Hamlets.

We totalled fifty scholastic novices, i.e. those intended for the
priesthood and about seven brother novices. The number varied
slightly as the occasional individual joined in the course of the

year or someone left. In my own year there were twenty-five of us, fourteen straight from school, the others ranging in age from nineteen to thirty-two. In the older group there were two school-masters, an ex-Anglican curate, a jeweller, a printer and a miner. The order of the day was largely that of the Tertians. We simply attended a mass, whereas they said and served one; we did not have to say office, but for one half hour every morning we peeled potatoes or did similar kitchen work while listening to Fr. Rodriguez' 'Practice of Perfection And Christian Virtue'. We also spent more time working in the grounds and we played mountain-side football. If the programme closely resembled that of the Tertianship, the atmosphere was very different. The mood was set by those straight from school. We were full of energy and what we mistook for zeal. The restrictions of our life funnelled our eagerness into our physical activities and we performed some of them at fanatical speed. We worked as though laying the cutlery one minute faster than usual would be a notable achievement for the Glory Of God. We swooped around the refectory as we served, scurried about the pantry and sometimes worked in the garden as though trying to save lives. I remember one fellow novice fervently digging up cabbage stalks and missing his target. He drove the nine inch tines through his boot into his foot. That was the extreme and not the norm, but the norm could be very hectic. It was in no way set by the Novicemaster, but had evolved from an amalgam of youthful zest with an idealism which had no proper target. The older men, especially those who were accus-tomed to physical labour, worked at a much more reasonable, human rhythm.

The Novicemaster, as new to his post as I to the noviceship, was Fr. Edward Enright. He was approaching forty-six and had been in charge of the Philosophers at Heythrop. He was a good pedagogue of a somewhat governessy kind. His instructions on the Society were beautifully lucid, his talks during the Long Retreat to the point and moving. Large though our number was, he saw us regularly and initiated us into the 'schola affectus'. Assessing in later years that introduction I felt that he overstressed self-scrutiny, as though our own perfection rather than the love of God was the primary focus. In matters of discipline he lacked a sense of proportion. His ideal young Jesuit always seemed to me too close to an old-fashioned schoolmistress's dream of a model

schoolboy. He taught us a great deal, but did not set us on the
path to maturity.

Circumstances were against him and us. The 'experiments' to
which the early generations were exposed were six. A novice had
to make the Spiritual Exercises for thirty days, which he would
have done by means of a single daily interview with the director.
Secondly, he had to work for a month in a 'xenodochium'. I
hesitate to translate that word as 'hospital' with its overtones of
order and antisepsis. The conditions of a sixteenth century hostel
with its uprooted, its aged and ill were the very opposite. Another
month was to be spent on pilgrimage. This was no Wandervogel
hiking holiday. The novices were sent out penniless, having to beg
their way 'so that they may get used to hardship of both bed and
board'. Fourthly, the novice had to take on a variety of 'humble
and lowly offices' and perform them with good grace. Fifthly, he
was to try his hand at teaching Christian doctrine to the 'unedu-
cated', a word which we apply to those who left school at fifteen.
Ignatius' novice was asked to cope with the wholly illiterate. To
get the flavour of those early noviceships we have to imagine the
graduate of perhaps Paris or Salamanca, who could have landed
himself a nice benefice, sent to beg his way along a sixteenth
century pilgrimage route, put to work for a month in some
reeking, utterly insanitary refuge and told to explain the Faith to
the abysmally ignorant. And in between these adventures he
performed domestic chore after domestic chore, when he had once
thought that his education and clerical status entitled him to be waited on for the rest of his life. These experiments were to be repeated
during the Tertianship, at the discretion of the Tertianmaster.

We as novices made the Long Retreat, but, of course, with little
personal direction. We performed 'lowly offices' such as sweeping
and scrubbing floors, which was no doubt salutary, but rather
less so for us than it would have been for our sixteenth century predecessors. And that was all out of six experiments! At
Roehampton the novices had 'catechised' Catholic schoolchildren,
but they were very scarce in Tremeirchion. So our exposure was
minimal. Our great 'experiment' was, as with the Tertianship later,
living patiently with our seclusion and a host of restrictions.
Because the country was at war the Novicemaster used to read a
selection of the daily news bulletins to us. In this respect we were
better off as novices than as tertians.

The second year, 1940-41, saw the brief return of the Tertianship to share the building with us. This was physically possible because the 1940 intake was small. In early 1941 both years added together only mustered twenty-eight scholastic novices and five brothers. There were twelve Tertians, all with one exception destined for overseas. Three were to go to Guiana, a Dutch Jesuit to Java and the others to Africa. Their Instructor was Fr. Bolland returning briefly to the post he had held before his Provincialate. We watched the Tertians with interest, but understood little. During their residence the intellectual quality of the refectory reading room rose notably under the influence of Fr. Bolland. I still remember a work about Ramon Lull, of whom I would otherwise never have heard, and long fascinating extracts from 'The Confessions' of Augustine. At the beginning of Lent the Tertians disappeared to their Lenten missions not to reassemble and we had St. Beuno's to ourselves once again. That was to change in the autumn when the Juniorate came to St. Beuno's, but by that time I was a Junior myself.

XIII

Rhetoric, restoration and radical reappraisal

On October 10th, 1940 Manresa House, Roehampton was hit during an air raid and Robert Howarth, who had taken his vows a month before at St. Beuno's was killed by a falling beam. The Juniorate, which had remained at Roehampton when the Novices had been despatched to Wales, was then transferred to Glasgow and in the following year to St. Beuno's. The house was not crowded. During the year 1941-42 the number of Novices hovered around twenty-six, and only six Juniors came from Glasgow to begin their second year Juniorate. Eleven of my own contemporaries formed the first year, seven older men going straight to Heythrop.

As Juniors, since we had taken vows, we wore full clerical clothes and had large birettas which we wore in the refectory, and which, if my memory is accurate, we carried to Chapel like Oxford undergraduates toting their mortarboards to examinations. We might have looked very dignified if we had been a few years older, but full clerical rig sat rather unconvincingly on a fresh-faced nineteen year old. I well remember our first talk from Fr. Thomas Corbishley, who had charge of us, exhorting us not to walk about in front of the Novices looking emancipated with our birettas on the back of our heads. We lived a wholly separate life, with our own work and our own recreations. Not for us evening meditation, peeling potatoes and sweeping the corridors. We did serve in the refectory and take our turn at reading during meals and delivering practice sermons as alternative fare. As a first year Novice I had not been allowed to preach during supper, since my thick scouse (Liverpool) accent was judged indigestible. As a second year Junior I was chosen to deliver the annual Latin panegyric on St. Aloysius, and for eighteen minutes at dinner boomed purple Latin into the rafters without any use of notes. I felt that I had made progress.

Officially we were Auditores Rhetoricae or Students of Rhetoric, the people G.M.H. had taught during 1873-74. In deference to the original title and its origins there was an elocution practice once a week, but without expert tuition. It was on one such occasion that I tried to recite the whole of the 'Lycidas', but needed a lot of prompting. There were two excellent periods of 'voice production', really singing practice, with Fr. O'Connor, who had the not uncommon combination of mathematical talent and musical ability. We had one lesson a week named 'English Essay' and wrote a fortnightly essay or sometimes a short story or even a longish literary essay to be read in class. This book could be traced back to those classes. The bulk of the time went on main line study. We revived our knowledge of Latin and French. We learned Greek and half of us, including myself, attended maths classes. There was a beginners' class in German and I spent quite a lot of time reading History and English Literature, but without tuition.

Our studies suffered to some extent from the same weakness which affected most of our formation, the bias towards mass production. More personal tuition, more setting of individual targets—perfectly feasible with our small numbers—would have paid large dividends. As it was, people who had successfully finished a Sixth Form course in French or Latin could find themselves sharing a class with those who had failed the subject at Fifth Form level, covering the same matter at the same rate. The teaching was good. Fr. Thomas Corbishley and Fr. Edmund D'Arcy were highly competent Classics scholars. Fr. Corbishley, not yet forty, was vivid, stimulating and unstarched. He lit a small flame of liberal Catholicism in me, which I hope never to let go out. Fr. D'Arcy was of an older generation, the impeccable scholar, the punctilious gentleman but of strong, if controlled feelings. He could without a word establish an atmosphere in which one felt that only one's very best work could be offered to this man without insult to his quality. The standard of the short stories and literary essays produced in the class was astonishingly high. It was a pedagogic achievement of which I have often dreamed, knowing I could never reproduce it. Fr. Edward O'Connor, the only man to have been Rector of Stonyhurst for two full terms of office, was with his Double First as well qualified in Mathematics as his colleagues in Classics. He fascinated me in Calculus and lost me, though not my two companions, in Co-ordinate Geometry. Fr.

Joseph Parsons, not by any means out of the same stable, did a workmanlike job of teaching French grammar and French prose. I left the Juniorate able to read Latin and French with ease, having learned a good deal of Greek and German grammar without the vocabulary to support it, with an outline knowledge of European history from Knossos to the First World War and having read all the Canterbury Tales and a great deal of nineteenth century literature. I could have been led into more exigent forms of study, but had much to be grateful for.

We also staged debates, took turns to give lectures and with the Novices for audience put on concerts and playlets. More ambitiously, in our second year, Fr. Corbishley decided to produce 'Julius Caesar', although there were only nine of us, himself playing Brutus. I was Caesar. It was rather frightening having a scrum of people plunging wooden daggers at one, but I emerged from a score of assassination rehearsals unscathed, while every conspirator had at least one long abrasion down his arm. When there were seventeen of us we could manage a game of football with the help of the younger laybrothers. Three cricket fanatics spent the free afternoons of the winter and spring laying a wicket on the hillside, which was used twice. In the second year nine of us could hardly manage team games. We worked in the garden for the sake of exercise rather than as a 'lowly office' and sometimes spent a few days on the farm helping to get in the potatoes or the hay. I remember stooking the corn so that it could arise 'barbarous in beauty', which was not the farmer's primary concern. On Sunday some of us rode out on bicycles to visit and 'catechise' Catholic evacuees. It was a very pleasant time, save that we were conscious that while we lived a rather schoolboy existence, our contemporaries were dying on land and sea and in the air.

During 1943-44 there were 12 Juniors and 26 Novices. In 1944 St. Beuno's became for a year a three-tier house of formation with nineteen Novices under Fr. Hugh Lyons, fourteen Juniors and a restored Tertianship under the legendary Fr. Keane. In 1945 the Noviceship returned to Roehampton leaving the house to 13 Juniors and 21 Tertians. In 1946 the Juniors followed the Novices to Roehampton and 36 Tertians had the house to themselves. The 'status quo ante bellum' had been restored.

The Juniorate no longer exists in the British Province, its Novices rarely, if at all, coming straight from school. Between 1982 and 1988 their average age was roughly twenty-five. Their smaller numbers have made it possible to abandon the conveyor belt processing from which previous generations suffered, and to give them the individual formation which the authentic tradition of the Society requires. A Novice is now guided individually through the Spiritual Exercises and the original 'experiments' have as far as possible been restored. Novices go on pilgrimage, not begging their way, but with camping equipment and slender resources. They are sent into refuges and hostels for the homeless, help in parishes and schools, doing so over a reasonably long period of time. More recently, the Novices have gone home at Christmas time and taken part in residential courses with the Novices of other congregations, many of them women. These two developments were definitely not in vogue in the early Society, but represent the conditions under which a Jesuit of the future is likely to live, having far more contact with his family, and working alongside and on equal terms with women.

Quite 'else-minded' was Fr. Keane, the dominating figure of the resuscitated Tertianship. He was Instructor from 1944 to 1947. In November of the latter year he was appointed Rector with Fr. Francis Mangan as Instructor, but when Fr. Mangan broke down at the end of the year, Fr. Keane picked up the baton, or rather the Epitome for another two laps. During 1948-49 he was both Rector and Instructor. In 1949 Fr. Neary of the Irish Province was Instructor; in 1950 Fr. Paul Whittaker became Vice-Rector, with Fr. Keane persevering as Instructor, until the death of Fr. Whittaker in January obliged him to fill both offices again. Fr. William d'Andria was Instructor in the following year, a rather odd appointment. He had been a highly successful parish priest and had given many retreats, but as a superior often lapsed into uncouthness and unpredictable irascibility with his Jesuit subjects. In 1952 the Instructor was Fr. Edward Helsham, who was ill in his first term, obliging Fr. Keane to give the Long Retreat yet again. He continued as Rector until January 1954 when he was replaced by Fr. Leo O'Hea.

In 1943, as a Philosopher at Heythrop, I heard Fr. Keane, then Rector, give a domestic exhortation. It was very impressive. In 1952 as Beadle of Theologians I read out of interest the entries of 1942-43 in the Beadle's Log. One day Fr. Keane had issued a series of decrees tightening the discipline of the house. Reading between the lines I could sense my predecessor's incredulity giving way to dismay as he realised that Fr. Keane meant every word of it. There one has the two sides of Henry Keane. There were people who were much moved by his deep religious sincerity. There were others who bristled at his name because they found him so rigid, so unbending. His career was remarkable. Joining the Society at seventeen, he was thirty-two before beginning Theology, thirty-seven when he finished his own Tertianship. Twenty years of 'formation' may account for much in his outlook. He was Prefect of Studies at Mount St. Mary's, Superior of the Philosophers, Master of Campion Hall, Provincial for eight years and then Provincial of Upper Canada for four. He became Instructor in 1938, held that office in Ireland until 1942 and was then Rector of Heythrop until 1944, when he again became Instructor. The Instructors of this period are mostly ex-Provincials, showing, I think, that they were chosen for their knowledge of the practical working of the Society rather than for their skill in the 'schola affectus'. As Fr. Keane gave excellent retreat conferences he may have seemed highly endowed in both spheres, but for some that endowment was entirely negated by what they saw as a bleak, unyielding rule by the book.

There was nothing bleak about Edward Helsham, who was Instructor from 1952 to '55. He had taught Theology, been Rector of Heythrop twice and Provincial briefly from 1950 to 1952. He was greatly respected and very much liked. It has been said that he was already a tired man when he became Provincial, and certainly by early '54 he was a sick man. His period as Instructor, while humane, was not likely to light any fires. Nor was the Tertianship directed by Fr. Francis Mangan (1955-58). He had been Novicemaster and was Provincial during the war. His rectitude, his sincerity, his deep personal piety were beyond question. He was shrewd, practical and even humorous and affectionate, but the humour was allowed very little play and the affection even less. One group of young men under his aegis substituted for Francis Mangan the label 'Frosty' Mangan.

Looking back on my own Tertianship under Fr. Mangan, and remembering all I ever heard said about their own from other men of my generation and before, it seems to me that for decades the English Province Tertianship lacked any dynamic. Both Instructors and Tertians went through the rituals, the Instructors with scrupulous conscientiousness, the Tertians with varying degrees of resignation. There is some bitterness and yet much objectivity in the comment, 'formation through stagnation', and a little more resentment in the remark, 'only the unashamedly pious and the unblushingly idle were really happy'. Disgust reached its zenith and objectivity almost, though not quite, disappeared in the verdict, wickedly reft from the Catechism, 'idleness, bad company and the neglect of prayer'.

Onto this barren terrain there was diverted in 1958 a stream from a seemingly quite inappropriate source, which was to irrigate and transform the whole landscape. Instructors were, as we have seen, commonly ex-Provincials. They were expected to have a fund of experience as superiors of the workings of the Society. Paul Kennedy had never held any position of authority whatsoever. Having completed the 'Longs' course but failed in the final exam he was not a Professed Father, but in the language of an earlier generation, one of the 'cab horses' of the Province. After his Tertianship he worked as a schoolmaster at St. Ignatius, Stamford Hill. He showed himself to be something of a spiritual maverick by trying the life of the Carthusians for a couple of months, but deciding that he should remain in the Society and so returning to his teaching post. He had taught there for seventeen years, when in 1954 he was sent to be Spiritual Father and one of the lecturers at Manresa Training College, Roehampton, which at that time held the Third Year Philosophers and those who stayed for a further year of Pedagogy in order to become certificated teachers. In late 1957 he went to St. Beuno's at twenty-four hours notice to help Fr. Mangan with the Long Retreat. This experience convinced him that he was quite unsuitable for such work and he provided the Provincial with a long list of the reasons why. During the summer he was giving a thirty-days retreat to the De La Salle Brothers, when he was informed that the General had appointed him Instructor. He managed to get to St. Beuno's eight days before the Tertians and greeted them with a wholly sincere cri de coeur, "My dear Fathers: the cupboard is bare'.

Paul did not claim to have even five loaves and two fishes, yet he was to nourish the Tertians from 1958 till 1974 as they had never been nourished at St. Beuno's before. Nor did the bread which he broke limit itself to St. Beuno's, nor to the period of his residence here. It continues to multiply both here and abroad. The year by year story of his transformation of the Tertianship and the later unfolding of his work would make a book of itself. This outstanding achievement was effected in highly unfavourable circumstances. He had first of all, as he had admitted, to contend with his own technical ignorance. Although keenly interested in 'spirituality', he was no specialist in that field, and the niceties of the Constitutions had never been his cup of tea. He had therefore to work out for himself what a Jesuit Tertianship should be aiming at and what methods, what activities, what sort of regime would best serve to accomplish those aims.

He soon saw the need to alter the structure of the Tertian's way of life, which meant altering many of the rhythms of the house and also carrying out physical changes. Here he met entrenched opposition and insuperable lack of imagination in Rectors, officals and the retired. His first Rector, Fr. Leo O'Hea, was from many points of view a saintly genius. He was rightly venerated in the Catholic Social Guild for his twenty-five years as its secretary and his thirty-two years as Principal of the Catholic Workers College. He was also an ornithologist of distinction, for whom it has been claimed that he knew more about birdsong than any other man in Europe. He was unassuming, deeply devout and possessed of extraordinary physical energy. Unfortunately, he was already seventy-seven when Paul came and seems to have been quite unable to grasp what the new Tertianmaster was aiming at or to see anything desirable in the changes proposed. To him and to the older members of the house, some of whom were consultors, the mechanics of the Tertianship, its noviceship order of the day, its noviceship restrictions, its insulation and in some respects its inertia, were all sacrosanct as part of the consecrated process by which the spiritual benefits of the Tertianship were invisibly harvested. They were horrified by any radical changes and opposed whatever alterations in the daily life of the house or its physical equipment those changes entailed. Apparently Fr. O'Hea saw himself as able not only to resist proposed modifications of the house's rhythms and its furnishings, but also to veto changes in matters which were purely internal to the Tertianship. Even the explicit and repeated intervention of the Provincial, who seems to have given Paul firm backing throughout, was often without effect. With some of the retired old gentlemen of the house the shocked expression of their consternation and disapproval became something of a hobby. In 1961 Fr. O'Hea was succeeded by Fr. Joseph Bickerstaff. Aged sixty-nine, he had been in office almost continuously since 1933 as Rector or Superior. He appears to have been less obstructionist than Fr. O'Hea and to have attempted to mediate between Paul and the scandalised seniors, but with little effect.

In his own account of his battlings Paul makes no mention of Rome, so I presume that nothing was done in that quarter to impede his schemes. In 1960 there was a suggestion that he be raised to the grade of Professed Father, to which Rome demurred. In 1967, after nine years of his striving with the senior establishment in the house, he was given overall control, but only as Vice-Rector, under which title he continued until his departure in 1974. Whether these two slights, if the title of Vice-Rector was a slight, indicate some ambivalence in the highest quarters, I cannot say.

The Tertians themselves were not always eagerly co-operative. A survey in the United States found that the Tertianship was commonly thought to be the least effective part of the Society's training, which hardly gave a new Instructor a good start with his American recruits. The largest contingent, the English, might arrive jaded and even somewhat recalcitrant, for their seventeenth year of pupillage. Some men from overseas were chiefly interested in seeing Europe; others had come largely to master English. The Tertianship, its individual activities, the instructor's decisions had all to be 'sold' to them. In the later stages of his Instructorship rising expectations, the turbulent wake of Vatican II and the continuing seismic tremors of 1968/9 provided quite a different set of difficulties from those of his starting years. Other difficulties stemmed from Paul's own person. To some temperaments his eccentricities were not easily digestible. To the highly organised he could seem unbearably chaotic. Becoming anxious about his heart condition he forswore baths and declined the alternative of the shower because of the risk of slipping. For years he would not go near the dentist, and so grinned at everyone with yellow fangs. His performances as lecturer and conferencier could swing between extremes. It has been said that on a good day he was the best speaker you had ever listened to and on a bad day the worst teacher you had ever encountered. His lively response to individuals sometimes led to the charge that his interest and concern were not impartially spread, not evenly offered to all.

In the face of all these difficulties, starting with little relevant experience and no expert knowledge Paul did two things. He revised the Tertianship radically and he set St. Beuno's on its present course. He began, as we saw, by avowing his own resourcelessness with the directness of the boy who saw that the Emperor had no clothes on. The boy, luckily for him, was not responsible for dressing the Emperor, but Paul was obliged to kit out an average of thirty Tertians a year for the next ten years and then the smaller groups of 1968-74. He studied the early Society and especially the first documents about the Tertianship. He asked himself about the application of what he found there to modern circumstances. He came to the conclusion that the Jesuit of the future would have to operate more like a guerilla fighter than as a soldier in the ranks, and that he would therefore need greater initiative and much more individual responsibility than his predecessors of the nineteenth and early twentieth centuries. It was important, then, that the Tertianship be something that the Tertian did for himself, just as it is the retreatant who makes the Exercises. The experiments were of the first importance and should be carefully arranged for each man. By the same token it was desirable that the Tertian decide the structure of his day for himself in consultation with the Director, but in such a way as not to cut across the common pattern of community activities. The primary task of the Tertian ought to be to find the will of God in his everyday life, and the purpose of the 'schola affectus' is to give him the requisite internal freedom, the clear-sightedness, the detachment of mind and heart which that search demands. The way of life of the Tertian should not be, if possible, abruptly different from that of the previous year, nor be in too sharp a contrast with the year to come.

One of Paul's first moves was to provide a good library. He toured France collecting titles and advice. The Province backed him quite generously. He made a special point of providing good periodicals. His chief difficulty came in getting a suitable room set aside and it was secured only after a war of attrition with the Rector. He got rid of the Custom book, which, couched in the same language as the Custom Book of the Noviceship, gave the Tertianship right from the start the same air of minute regimentation from which the Noviceship suffered, and which had ceased to be appropriate even there. The Tertians were no longer turned out to work in the gardens. Paul sought out 'experiments' for them in hospices, borstals, Cheshire homes and temporary chaplaincies in prisons and military bases.

Looking through the Tertians' Log of the early seventies I see as much resemblance between my Tertianship and theirs as between Eohippus and the two Shire horses which graze in the Rock Chapel field, but with the evolution of the Tertianship under Paul Kennedy taking hardly more than a dozen years. In September '71 I read of the Tertians meeting to discuss what the regular order of their day should be. Gone the long timetable which told us when to do 'By Heart' and when to say Vespers. On January 6th '74, Paul spoke of the impending study of the Constitutions. He proposed to give two talks a day with a question-and-answer session in the evening. The Tertians talked him out of the evening session in order, in the Beadle's words, to protect 'the sacred hour of TV viewing'. We left St. Beuno's, not for the whole of Lent, but only for one month of it and after Easter two people went each weekend to help in the retreat house outside Liverpool. Paul's Tertians not only went on the traditional Lenten missions, they went out for Advent and Christmas. In '71 they disappeared on December 3rd 'to destinations between Glasgow and Gibraltar' to reassemble on January 10th. In April there was an eight day conference held at Campion House, Osterley, with eleven speakers, including Shirley Williams M.P. and Dr. Dominian, the celebrated psychiatrist. The log also shows people departing in twos or singly on other 'experiments'. One did a flying course. Another helped to edit the Province magazine 'The Month'. There were many weekend supplies. Daily concelebration, sometimes at midday or in the evening, replaced the early morning pairing of 'say a mass; serve a mass'.

Numbers did not allow the Long Retreat to be 'directed' i.e. with the material chosen for each individual each day and talked over in a daily interview. Paul compromised, reducing the talks to two a day, one during the Third Week (The Passion), and making his way round to see the exercitants perhaps every other day. After the retreat he allowed some days for reflection and then arranged for several days of study and group discussions. It was in the sphere of the Exercises together with that of spiritual

direction in general that he appears to have been most effective.
Fr. Howard Gray, Provincial of Detroit, says, 'he brought us (the
American Jesuits) close to the experience of the Exercises. He gave
us a belief in the power of informed spiritual direction'. Some of
the leading Transatlantic figures in the study and presentation of
the Exercises were Tertians at St. Beuno's. They include John
English of Canada (1962-63), who was to be the Director of
that Mecca of Ignatian spirituality, Loyola House, Guelph, Ontario,
George Schemel of Maryland (1965-66) who directed a similar
institution, the Jesuit Center for Spiritual Growth at Wernersville,
Pennsylvania and David Fleming of Missouri (1966-67) who was to
translate the Exercises anew and himself become a Tertian Instructor. Paul had a strong affection for the Americans. Fr. Gray says,
'He had a sensitive regard for North American customs, but a
shrewd ability to help us see these as one way to live not the only
way to live. Paul . . . taught us how to listen to the people we
served and how to learn from and with them'. One of the things
he learned from his Americans was an appreciation of American
football, which in his retirement 'he faithfully followed on TV
whenever it was available.' It says much for Paul's handling of
people and his sympathetic respect for varying cultures that the
Australians, no less than the Americans, considered him to be
particularly close to themselves. Fr. John Eddy (1967-68) writes,
'there was a special rapport and continuity in his relations with
the Australians which both recognised. We adopted him and he
adopted us'. Two other tributes to Paul I should like to quote: 'He
was remarkably intuitive with individuals' and 'He was very good
with men who were hanging on by their fingertips'.

After weighing such citations, talking to some of his Tertians
and reading his reflections on the Tertianship, my own respect
goes out to him on two grounds particularly, his honesty and his
sense of history. He was honest about himself and also, which
was much rarer, honest about the Society's techniques of formation wherever they seemed ineffective in the present. The men
responsible for my own formation believed, it seemed, that the
Society's way as practised in our own time and in the English
Province were a priori excellent, and that when they did not
succeed it was because of the defective co-operation of individual
Jesuits. My Tertian Instructor allowed himself one admission.
Returning from a conference of Instructors he told us that the

Instructor of Province after Province had declared that he emphasised to his Tertians the crucial importance of the traditional pattern of 'spiritual' duties, knowing full well that in a few months the men would be far too busy to keep to them. Having delivered this torpedo to the craft on which we were supposed to sail for the rest of our lives, he did not offer us the lifebelt of a single suggestion as to how we were to keep afloat in the coming flood.

Commending his sense of history, I am not implying that Paul had any detailed knowledge of past events. I mean that he realised that the usages of yesterday have not necessarily been there from the beginning, that they may not serve all the needs of today, and even less those of tomorrow. The conservative, who has no sense of history, wants today and tomorrow to be exactly like yesterday, not realising that yesterday was in many respects quite different from the day before. In consequence he can find himself defending as 'traditional' and conferring a more or less sempiternal value on some practice which is in historical terms comparatively recent. Paul sought solutions to the fundamental problems which met him by going back to the Society's origins and early developments, evaluating present practices in the light of the original objectives and then trying to discern what methods might secure those aims in the future lives of his Tertians. Paul Kennedy did not need to set up his chair at the water's edge to learn that time and tide wait for no man, not even a Jesuit with the Epitome in his hand.

XIV

The Tower and the running tide

Paul Kennedy transformed more than the methods and mores of the Tertianship. He was responsible for the transformation of the interior of the building, although transformation may be too sweeping a word for the process of repair and modernisation, which beginning under Fr. Kennedy, continues today with a fresh burst of progress each mid-winter. In the early sixties there was question of moving the Tertianship elsewhere. What use the Province would have found for the house without the Tertians, I am unable to conjecture. Perhaps none. The Tertians stayed. Paul, having first toured the corresponding houses in France and surveyed the British alternatives to St. Beuno's decided to remain. His decision was ratified by the Canadian Visitor to the Province, Fr. Gordon George, who concluded a visitation to the Province in August 1965.

With his Olympian approbation there began an heroic effort to modernise a mid-Victorian building and repair the dilapidations of a hundred and twenty years. The operation was at times almost seismic in character. First, most of the roof had to be stripped and renewed. Then the entire central heating system was dismantled and another installed which covered the whole building. Hot and cold water was carried to each room and the whole electrical system renewed and considerably extended. The heating, the supply of both hot and cold water, the waste from the basins and the additional wire all needed pipes of appropriate size to pass through the old walls, most of which were 23 inches thick. The noise and the dust I can imagine, having experienced the comparatively small scale modifications of succeeding Januaries. The stairs, worn down by more than a century's pounding by brisk young feet, needed to be renewed and the old fireplaces had to be blocked. The builders were followed by the joiners, the joiners by the painters.

The renovation of the structure was followed by improved furnishing, although to a limited extent. Concelebrated masses meant changes in the Chapel. The centre aisle was raised to the height of the floor on either side and the ancient benches replaced by chairs so, said Fr. Kennedy, that you could pick up your chair and put it where you could pray best. The benches in the Chapel were less primitive than those in the lecture room. These massive objects stretched almost from wall to wall, were of thick wood and rested on cast iron stanchions which were screwed to the floor. They looked more like anti-tank defences than educational furnishings. Paul replaced them by individual tables of very light build, trapezoid in shape, ingeniously designed so that they could be assembled in a variety of formations, as required. The antique iron bedsteads went.

The process was given a further nudge forward as the house prepared to receive nuns on retreat. The Notre Dame Provincial, Sister Mary Consuela, urged curtains to replace the roller blinds and dusty swathes of blackout material, the provision of utility rooms with kettles and ironing boards and something other for refectory use than 'those British Rail' cups and saucers and heavy duty plates. In 1972 the kitchen was overhauled. In 1976 the refectory lost its monastic air, the tables no longer running along the walls so that the diners faced one another across the room, and new tables and chairs give it the look of a dining room in a well conducted school. The pulpit from which generations of Jesuits read and preached above the rattle of crockery and the thud of servers' feet, now holds a record player to decant 'magic numbers and persuasive sound' over the heads of feeding exercitants. In the same year the bare boards trodden by Gerard and myself ('nor can foot feel being shod'—Thank goodness!) began to disappear beneath linoleum. Some more years would elapse before carpeting appeared in private rooms.

The prompting of the nuns, and later of women directors, the opening up of the house to lay retreatants and the development of longer courses in the eighties, especially the Three Month Course, all kept the process of improvement in motion. You could not, for instance, expect people to accept for three months the austerities and inconveniences which they would endure for an eight days retreat. So, more showers, bathrooms, lavatories, improved laundry facilities, some double glazing, the addition of wardrobes and bedside cabinets and the refurnishing of public rooms. The galleries and stairs have been affected by the modifications required by modern fire regulations. There are fire doors every-where, two new staircases provide alternative routes from Attica and Priests Gallery and fire screens break up the long vista of the galleries.

In the above chronicle of refurbishment I have let the tale of the effects outrun the story of their causes. In the sixties very little happened in the house during the long absences of the Tertians and in the long months of the summer. The clergy of Menevia and Shrewsbury held a couple of brief midweek retreats, a num-ber of Jesuits made their private retreats and there was, in the words of one of my informants, a product of Rugby and Oxford, 'nowt else'. Among Paul Kennedy's devoted friends were quite a number of women religious including Sister Dorothy Bell, Principal of Digby Stuart College of Education and Sister Mary Consuela, Provincial of the Sisters of Notre Dame de Namur. With the advice of these ladies Paul planned to open the house to women religious for retreats. The first was in July 1970. It was meant to last eight days, but Paul, about to celebrate mass on the 22nd said, 'Oh. Is it the feast of St. Mary Magdalen? I am going to the U.S. tomorrow', and the retreat ended a day early. The nuns found the place 'filthy' and a number of them could not resist the temptation to set about it. At dinner they were a little taken aback to be offered beer.

The next such event was an eight day retreat for Notre Dame Superiors in 1971. Again some of them could not resist trying to raise the standard of cleanliness from the near abysmal. They beat what bits of carpeting there were till they ceased to yield clouds of dust. The kneelers on their priedieus received the same treatment. They lined the drawers with newspaper. One nun was rather flung to find in a drawer a single dirty sock and an empty whisky bottle, the latter no doubt the relic of some clerical retreatant. She compulsively washed the sock and then consulted a more worldly wise colleague about the bottle. Her confidant's solution was to relieve her of the bottle, and in the course of a walk dispose of it in a hedge 'so that no-one would get into trouble'. In 1972 there was a full Thirty Days Retreat for women religious conducted by Paul with the assistance of Fr. George Earle. These retreats were what we would call 'semi-directed', with a single talk in the morning and a brief interview with the director every other day. Again 'seven maids with seven mops', or more accurately, a couple of dozen nuns with whatever dusters and implements they could find, tackled the rungs of chairs, the skirting boards and the jumbo-sized cobwebs. Throughout the retreat the old gentlemen beamed encouragement and the brothers showed themselves eager to be as helpful as possible, if a little bewildered by all this spring cleaning. The men began to learn. A sister making a retreat in 1973 found her room clean, an iron and kettle not far away and whatever else she had need of easy to find, while Brother Bruce had put flowers in all the rooms. It was outside of the bedrooms that the old standards, or the lack of them, still reigned. 'There didn't seem to be any cleaning'.

These Thirty Day retreats became an annual feature, the first fully directed retreat (i.e. with the director seeing his exercitant every day and selecting material for that individual) being given in 1976 by Fr. Earle, Sister Kathleen McGhee S.N.D. and Fr. William Hewett. By initiating these retreats Paul Kennedy had breached the unspoken assumption that the house was open only to Jesuits and diocesan priests. Where the nuns had come the laity would follow, as they were to do in such numbers in the years ahead. In fact, there was a laywoman on the 1972 retreat, Mrs. Pauline King of Bath. With women coming on retreat it made sense to employ women in the house. In 1972 Mrs. Margaret Mercer was taken on to work in the scullery, a post quite out of sight of both residents and retreatants. 'Maggie' was nevertheless, quite unconsciously the vanguard of a regiment. Mrs. Elsie Edwards, the wife of the cook 'Bert' Edwards, who has himself given St. Beuno's more than fifty years of sterling service, was the second woman employee. She supervised the dining room and helped with the sick. Within a few years women would take over the kitchen and the cleaning and after that the office administration. In 1976 as we have seen, Sister McGhee directed a retreat. By the mid eighties women directors would outnumber the men on the summer retreats and be members of the 'permanent' team.

Another move made in the seventies proved rather abortive. When I was a first year Novice the house contained six old men listed as 'cur. val.' (invalids). In 1948 the term was replaced by the more positive description 'orat pro Soc.' i.e. 'praying for the Society'. During my Tertianship there were only three so described, which was deceptive, as there were others old and ill, but with some very light responsibility such as 'house confessor', of

which there were several. Consequently, I have always thought of
St. Beuno's as having its group of retired and infirm, an impression which the house lists do not wholly confirm. In the first
thirty years an invalid member of the community is rare. It is
when we come to the eighties of the last century that we find
three men designated 'cur. val.' After that there is more often only
one, occasionally two, rarely three, and from 1912 till 1920 there
are none at all. It is after the house becomes a Tertianship that it
normally contains a group of invalids 'praying for the Society'.
These old men, with a dedicated life behind them and preparing
for eternity in front of them, are a not negligible strand in the
history of the house over the last sixty years, one not to be
forgotten, I think, by the retreatant praying over his or her own
life.

Far from forgetting its old men, the English Province in the
nineteen sixties was worrying about them. Everyone, including
Jesuits, were living longer and in common with all other congregations, the Province was asking itself where they could best be
housed. In 1971 there arrived at St. Beuno's Brother James Spence,
a highly qualified nurse. He brought professional standards to
bear. He asked for improved facilities. A dispensary was established, a sluice room and a bathroom specially fitted for an invalid.
Visiting the house in 1972 and seeing Brother Spence at work, I
felt quite reassured about my own twilight years. I was over-
optimistic. Brother Spence left St. Beuno's in 1975. He reported to
the authorities that St. Beuno's did not seem to him a suitable
place for the retired. He argued that the old would feel too
isolated, too cut off, that there was no bus service and, from a
house built on Maenefa, few flat places where they could walk. If
St. Beuno's was being considered as a 'Province Infirmary', the
scheme was abandoned in 1975.

In the October of 1974 after sixteen years in which he had
introduced more changes into St. Beuno's than all his predecessors
put together, Paul Kennedy left, and Fr. Alphonse Pollet was
appointed Temporary Superior. In the Province Catalogue of 1975
St. Beuno's is described not only as a house of formation or
training, but as a retreat house. There was in fact no Tertianship
during that year. Of the eight priests over whom Fr. Pollet
presided, one was the Minister, another a 'supply priest' i.e.
helping out in parishes suddenly short of a priest. The other six

were 'praying for the Society'. The year could be little more than a holding operation. The improvements to the house continued and retreats were given. The Minister, Fr. Francis Collins, gave special attention to the garden. Today when I see red and white roses flowering among the fruit of an apple tree or a clematis strikingly in bloom upon a pear tree, I know that I am looking at some of Frank's imaginative handiwork.

In September 1975 Fr. Pollet was replaced by Fr. Michael O'Halloran, who was to stay only two years. His brief was to extend the retreat work and to look after the retired. During his first year there was no Tertianship for the second year running, but Fr. Thomas Northover arrived to help with the retreat work, in which Fr. McIlhenny also took part, although he was technically one of the retired. Michael made a special effort with the local clergy, religious and laity. Besides retreats he organised clergy days and prayer groups and held school retreats. He also paid attention to the house's connection with G.M.H. and organised a Hopkins weekend and celebrated the centenary of the poet's ordination. At the end of his second year in office he left for Rhodesia (Zimbabwe), having been appointed Rector of St. George's College, Salisbury (Harare). Once again St. Beuno's found itself with a temporary Superior, this time Fr. Thomas Lakeland.

Once again also, the sword of Damocles, which had been dangled over St. Beuno's as early as the eighteen fifties and as late as the nineteen sixties was sensed hovering again. Had it descended at this point the 'stroke of havoc' would have lopped off the most richly flowering branch that St. Beuno's ever put forth. It would also have spared me the most difficult of its decades to describe.

The branch of which I have just spoken with such enthusiasm had been engrafted in 1976 when another Tertianship gathered at St. Beuno's with Fr. Michael Ivens as Instructor and Fr. Gerard W. Hughes as Co-Instructor. Michael Ivens had worked in the Chaplaincy at Manchester University, been Spiritual Father at Campion Hall, Oxford and had assisted in the Editorship of 'The Way', a very successful review of Christian Spirituality, for six years. Gerry was the older man by nine years. He had been in charge of the Sixth Form at Stonyhurst and was an enterprising, popular and controversial University Chaplain at Glasgow. On leaving that appointment he had walked to Rome, subsequently publishing 'In Search Of A Way', which interweaves the actual walk with his own internal, spiritual and intellectual pilgrimage. Both Michael and Gerry were members of The Way Community, a rather misleading name for a group of six Jesuits and two women religious, Sister Kathleen McGhee S.N.D. and Sister Mary Grant (Sacred Heart Congregation) who concerned themselves with the knowledge and use of The Spiritual Exercises and the renewal of religious life in the light of the Second Vatican Council. Some members of the group had already directed retreats, especially the Thirty Day retreats, at St. Beuno's and now made their expertise available to the Tertianship. For their experiments the Tertians lived in self-catering groups, preferably in council flats, involved in schools and what could be broadly termed social work. In 1978 Gerry was appointed Superior, The Way Community having been dissolved that summer, and my difficult decade begins.

My difficulty is fourfold. First, to do justice to the imaginative developments of the last ten years would require a fair amount of detail, and I feel that the reader, having trudged mentally from Loyola to Liege and from the Lancashire Fells to the Clwydian Hills, and having watched the stage occupied by the Theologians, the Tertians, the Novices, the Juniors and the Tertians once again, does not want the final (?) transformation scene to be overlong. Secondly, the events are very close, not only in time but even physically, as I have been physically present here since January '85. Such proximity makes it difficult to see things in focus and to assess their relative significance. Thirdly, whereas the traditional, largely unchanging communities of the past kept detailed records of their doings, St. Beuno's post '78 has not even retained copies of the yearly list of events distributed for advertisement. Fourthly, the detached stance of judicious appraisal, necessary when one is trying to describe the past, becomes quite inappropriate when recounting the achievements of one's colleagues. Yet recounted they must be.

They must also in justice to the men of the past be put into their context. When Paul Kennedy had begun to introduce changes into the Tertianship he had run into the indignant criticism and conscientious opposition of those for whom the only way was the traditional way, shallow though the roots of those particular traditions might be. When he came to lay down office he had for some time been defending himself on the opposite flank, trying to contain the impatience and frustration of those for whom his many adaptations did not go far enough. It was a situation shared by many another pioneer reformer of the sixties later caught in the slipstream of the Second Vatican Council, a slipstream at times of hurricane force.

In Janary 1959 Pope John XXIII had announced that he was calling an Ecumenical or General Council. It is said that when asked why, he dramatically stalked across the room and in an acted parable threw open the window. The Council opened in October 1962 and the strength of the breeze which blew through the open casement was to take everyone by surprise. It blew, not from any one direction, but collected its force from a variety of sources. One was the vigorous and far reaching revival of Scripture studies among Catholics, which inevitably led to a distinct shift of theological and ecclesiastical perspective. Another was the catechetical movement which had ceased to offer converts and children the abstractions and technicalities of a diluted seminary course, but sought for something far more personal, experiential and concrete with which to express the Faith. The liturgical movement, which admittedly dates back to the nineteenth century, had become far more pastorally orientated, far less concerned with rubrical exactness and the aesthetics of a bygone age, and more intent on participation and pedagogic effectiveness. At the same time theologians such as Congar, de Lubac and Rahner were expressing theology in a very different fashion from the 'uninspired Scholastic Aristotelianism' which had ruled the seminary roost so long. The ecumenical movement was stimulating at least some Catholics to consider far more sympathetically the faith and worship of other Christians and so to reflect much more sensitively on their own. I myself consider that there was another factor involved (which I have never seen invoked by another writer) and which I offer to the judgement of the reader. Catholics reared in parliamentary democracies had lived too long with a contradiction between their lives as citizens and as members of the Church. As democrats we believed in free speech, a free press, representative institutions and the accountability of government. As Catholics we lived with tight censorship, an Index of Forbidden Books of alarming comprehensiveness and an ecclesiastical system which was extremely centralised, wholly autocratic and quite beyond our questioning. We yearned for the anomaly to be at least mitigated. Perhaps the most pervasive infiuence of all was the visionary optimism of Teilhard de Chardin, which challenged the Church to come out from behind its multiple defences and embrace in love, humility and confidence the world which God had made and for which Christ had died.

It came—or at least a majority of its bishops came—a surprisingly long way out. The liturgy was transformed, the Latin monopoly which had endured a millennium and a half and been imposed upon Eskimo, Samoan and Hottentot alike, received its quietus. The great documents were based on Scripture, showed a sense of history, had a strong pastoral flavour and were wholly different in tone from the 'timeless' Neoscholastic terminology we had come to expect. The declarations on Religious Freedom and Non-Christians showed nothing of the old defensiveness and in the decree on Ecumenism the Council took a stance both contrite and humble. The fundamental document, that on The Church, focusing at an early stage on 'the college or body of the bishops' as 'expressing the variety and universality of the People of God', modified, at least in theory, the absolute Vaticanism of the previous ninety years. The same document dealt clericalism something of a body blow by devoting the whole of its fourth chapter out of the eight to the subject of The Laity, while the priests were covered in a single section out of sixty-nine. In the document on 'Religious Life' the Council defined 'appropriate renewal' of orders and congregations as having 'two simultaneous processes', the first, 'a continuous return to the sources of all Christian life and to the original inspiration behind a given community' and the second, 'an adjustment of the community to the changed condition of the time'. This was exactly Paul Kennedy's approach to the reinvigoration of the Tertianship.

Here it is not my task to expound the theological achievement of the Council, but merely to indicate its relevance to a developing St. Beuno's. The chief effect of the Council on the house was that change could no longer be treated as 'untraditional' and therefore suspect and probably pernicious. By the time the Council closed in December 1965 'renewal', 'adaptation' and—I must use the word at last—'aggiornomento' were the badges of apostolicity. It was a heady period when we seemed to be advancing towards the Kingdom in seven league boots. Nostalgia wells up within me as I write. In 1968 the French students took to the streets and almost toppled De Gaulle from power. Throughout the Western world there were campus demonstrations and 'sit-ins'. It was the day of the hippy, of flower power and multiplying communes. I found myself having to rethink almost every aspect of my life, the nature of the Church, the essence of the Christian ministry, the shape of our rituals, the purposes of a school and the methods appropriate to them. In January '68 I was Fr. Edwards, a cleric in a long black gown, a Deputy-Head who knew that a sixthformer's hair should not stick over the back of his collar. By October '69 I had dropped the prefix 'Father', was called 'Paul' by almost everyone, and had bought a pair of warm, very comfortable, but quite graceless jeans. And I no longer knew how long or short anybody's hair should be. All of which metamorphosis was due, not, as the reader suspects, to a second adolescence, but to serious theological and social reflection. My jeans, worn during my sabbatical year at Bristol University, may seem out of place in a history of St. Beuno's. I wave them here in salute to those days when responsible freedom, creativity rooted in authentic tradition, a genuine openness and a warm universal solicitude appeared to bear us forward on an irresistible tide. Alas! We underestimated the need for profound humility and unremitting self-discipline, without which there is no lasting spiritual achievement.

Paul Kennedy inherited the rigid patterns of his predecessors, benefited from the Great Thaw of Vatican II and finally had to deal with the wet rush of facile over-optimism. Without the Great Thaw he would never have been able to open the house to women religious. His successors were in a position to exploit the change of climate much further. Michael Ivens and Gerard Hughes were both steeped in Vatican II. They had also, and I am sure this is important, been university chaplains in the heady days of '68 and '69. More important still was their membership of The Way Community, which concerned itself with the renewal of religious life in the light of Vatican II and still more with the Spiritual Exercises.

Vatican II and the reviviscence of the Spiritual Exercises are therefore an inextricable part of the development of St. Beuno's at this stage. Throughout my scholasticate the Exercises, even the full 'Thirty Days' were given to large numbers simultaneously. The director, in my earliest memories, gave five addresses each day, the exercitant praying privately after four of them. One address was called a 'conference' and was not matter for meditation. To their credit directors of the Thirty Days tried to keep in touch with individuals, giving brief interviews to each when and as they could. Those interviews, fitted into what was left of the days after the five talks, had necessarily to be quite far apart as well and briskly conducted. How many days did it take for Fr. Bolland to see his forty-two Tertians once? The eight day retreat, made annually by most congregations, might be given to as many as a hundred people together. For such a retreat the matter of the Exercises was shrunk to fit a quarter of its proper length. Unless the director was something of a maverick therefore the pattern of development was totally predictable.

It was a formula of which Ignatius had never dreamed. For the early Jesuits the Exercises were made once in a lifetime, and during them the director dealt with each retreatant singly seeing him or her once a day, setting out the matter for meditation concisely and with no more than minimum comment. This, the original form of the Exercises, revived in the sixties and seventies, came to be known as the 'directed retreat' as distinct from a 'preached retreat'. Obviously the directed retreat was, in the jargon of modern industry, 'labour intensive'. If the exercitant were to be visited daily and be given a reasonable amount of time in which to report and discuss the experience of the previous twenty-four hours, then a handful of retreatants would soon fill a director's day. The daily interview presented the director with the opportunity to guide the exercitant into a deeper, more fruitful experience of the Exercises than that offered by the preached retreat. It also raised the possibility that should he be clumsy or insensitive with the individual concerned, he might well do a great deal more harm than in a preached retreat. If the directed retreat were to become at all widely available, and safe into the bargain, then many more directors have to be far more carefully selected and trained than the givers of preached retreats . . . if the latter could truthfully be described as trained at all.

The provision of well trained directors has now become St. Beuno's principal objective. In 1978, however, the aims of the house were far less precisely focused. In the optimistic, globe-embracing spirit of Vatican II Gerard and Michael looked rather to find new areas to which they might bring spiritual inspiration and new methods of bringing it. The Council's blessing on renewal and adaptation brought them the cooperation of other religious willing to take up new work in different circumstances, while the decree On Ecumenism backed their efforts to bring other Christians into the ambit of their efforts. Even more influential, I think, was the Council's emphasis on the role of the laity in the Church, which coincided accidentally with the rise in Britain of a new large class of highly educated Catholics. When I was a teacher in my first year in 1946-47 the whole of our sixth form could be assembled in one of the smaller classrooms. By 1969 we had more than a hundred sixth formers, although we were drawing on a smaller catchment area than in '46 and sharing that smaller area with another Catholic grammar school which had an equal number of sixth form boys. The majority of those two hundred boys were going on to higher education, and in so doing they and their peers were decisively altering the character of the Catholic community at large. Such was the religious and social scene of the decade 1978-88, the achievements of which I must now summarise.

First, let us say farewell to the Tertians. Michael Ivens, who had already conducted three Tertianships for Brothers in England, Australia and Zimbabwe, agreed with the view of Paul Kennedy that the Tertianship is a community and not a place, and took the principle to a more practical conclusion. His Tertians spent only four months at St. Beuno's before going off to their council flats for their experiments. They then regathered for a period of assessment at Barmouth in the 'Villa' house to which that band of Theologians had marched more than a century before. During the Tertianship of 1979-80 Michael made up his mind quite firmly that St. Beuno's was no longer a suitable place for it. The Tertians, temporary sojourners within an established working community, felt themselves to be on the fringe of things, while on the other hand their presence restricted the scope of the house's expanding activities. Thenceforth Michael's formula was to find some suitable venue—no matter if it differed from year to year—for the opening part of the Tertianship concerned mostly with the Exercises, to send the men out on their individual experiments, and then to hold the third part of the Tertianship dealing with the Constitutions and related matters in another place altogether. A further inspiration of Michael's was to join forces with the Irish Province, and the more recent Tertianships have been joint Anglo-Irish affairs, run by Michael and Fr. Joseph Veale. The most recent began with two months in Ireland, continued with the individual experiments and finished with two months at Campion House, Osterley, for the Constitutions etc. But St. Beuno's sees the Tertians no more.

Other people it began to see in numbers and variety as never before. The decade 1978-88 comes more easily into focus, I find, when divided into two lustra (a practical, if slightly precious term) of '78-'83 and '83-'88. The first period, to judge by programmes and the accounts of people involved, was one of almost tropical growth, profuse, colourful, exuberantly fertile. The second lustrum is rather one of deliberate, methodical, efficient agriculture. Gerry Hughes' primary success, it seems to me, was his ability to attract men and women of calibre and experience to share the work and in the case of Jesuits to coax, or otherwise get them, from the Provincial Fr. William Maher. The first to join the staff was Fr. Fintan Creaven with his flair for and specialist training in visual presentation. He was followed in the next year, 1981, by Fr. David Townsend, a trained and experienced counsellor and Fr. William Broderick, who had been Rector at Enfield and Stonyhurst, and spent some time at Wernersville, a place already mentioned as directed by George Schemel, a Kennedy Tertian. In 1983 came Fr. David Brigstocke, our present Superior, a man who has studied the Rhineland mystics, belonged to an ashram in India, worked for two years in Pakistan and so built up a knowledge of spirituality outside the Ignatian and even outside the Christian tradition. Also, when I talk over this early period with those who took part in it, I hear the names of a whole procession of women retreat directors and other specialists from a variety of congregations, together with some laywomen.

It is interesting to study the programme of '79—a handful of programmes did turn up—and compare it with that of '81. In '79 the Tertians still required the use of much of the house and the services of Michael and Gerry for four months. Nevertheless, there were retreats for a wide variety of people, for the clergy, for religious, for the laity, for students and sixth formers. There was a course on the Spiritual Exercises by a Canadian, Fr. Cusson, and an 'Institute For Retreat Givers And Spiritual Directors'. This was really a Thirty Days Retreat with an introduction and a period of reflection afterwards, its importance being the quality of people whom it attracted. Many a visiting director says to me, 'I did the Institute in the early days'. Two years later in '81 the programme has burgeoned almost luxuriantly. It contained weekends on different aspects of prayer, and courses on counselling, the Easter Liturgy, R.E. teaching, Hopkins, the National Pastoral Congress and spiritual direction. There were workshops on retreat direction, a seminar on religious and priestly formation and another on the 16th century directories to the Exercises. There were two more 'Institutes' as described and a very impressive effort to reach out beyond the world of religious congregations and mainstream Catholicism with weekends for the divorced and separated and 'non-church-going Catholics' and a week for the deaf. A meeting of spiritual directors with psychologists and psychiatrists has become an annual event. Gerry brought in not only visiting directors and specialists from outside the ranks of Jesuitry, he attracted onto the staff both religious and lay people to work in the office and give general assistance. In January '83 he appointed a lay Bursar, Michael Scanlan.

In the course of that year Gerry laid down office and was succeeded as Superior by Fintan Creaven while the management of the retreat house was assigned to William Broderick as Director. This second lustrum develops the work of its predecessor with less pioneering and more consolidation. Common to both is the influence of John English, the Director of Loyola House, Guelf, already mentioned as one of Paul Kennedy's Tertians, who gave a workshop on retreat directing in '82 and a workshop on 'Christian Governance' in 1985, both of which courses have been adopted into our programme. Sister Pia I.B.V.M., the first resident woman director, and Sister Kathleen S.N.D. the second, had had part of their training at Guelf, and Gerry had been temporarily on their staff. Also common to both periods is the ecumenical dimension. David Brigstocke prides himself on having had five Anglican bishops among his retreatants. Anglicans and members of other denominations come on the Three Months Course (see below) and on some eight day retreats Papists barely muster a majority. It is a matter of course for there to be an Anglican director assisting on these retreats. I treasure the words of an Anglican Bishop to a prospective ordinand living in Clwyd, 'Make the most of St. Beuno's'.

In the autumn of '82 the Institute of Spirituality was extended to three months, incorporating with the full Exercises, the listening course, the Faith and Justice course and the Exercises workshop, which had been separate items. The label 'Institute' has been altered to 'Three Month Course in Spirituality' and is habitually referred to as the '3M'. There are two such courses a year, which with the full Exercises in the summer and the eight day retreats, leaves less time than formerly for the rich variety of courses offered by Gerry. There is less time to play with in the programme and less room in the house. It is no longer possible to invite people at short notice, or for them to invite themselves. Now retreats are fully booked early in the year and the 3M is full months before it begins. The present emphasis is on training directors. Promising people are invited to help on eight day retreats with guidance. Experienced eight day directors may then be invited to help with the full Exercises with supervision and instruction. I have been keenly aware during my five years residence of rising standards. I am conscious at our meetings of the staff's self-criticism, of their aspiration to an even higher level of competence.

The international aspect of the work I find very impressive. The 3M attracts people from every continent. Not only do we get missionaries from Japan, Indonesia, India, Africa and the West Indies, we get Japanese, Indonesians, Indians, Africans and West Indians. There are Americans and Australasians every time the course is held, but Latin Americans are somewhat rare. Europe has been represented by Germans, Dutch, Belgians, Spaniards, Poles and Frenchmen. The preoccupation with the 3M, with training and with raising our own competence has not caused us to lose sight of Gerry's aim to have a diversified staff. A married couple, Christopher and Mary Campbell-Johnston, now live with us, help with directions and assist with administration. We still try to reach out to the fringes of the Church. This year's programme contained a weekend, 'Facing Up To Aids in Years To Come'. It brought a small group of sufferers with their friends and pastors.

As I mistype this page two members of the staff, Sister Kathleen McGhee S.N.D. and Fr. Terry McGrath (Missionary of St. Francis de Sales) are supervising the full Exercises of thirty days. The team of directors consists of a Jesuit, two other priests, a Christian Brother, three women of different congregations and a laywoman. The Brother is directing a priest, a seminarist, a woman religious and a laywoman. It is not quite what Fr. Lythgoe had in mind as he came down Cwm hill.

Here I shall halt.

Conclusion

'Is the history of St. Beuno's a parable of wrong-headed resistance to the tide of change, or is it an inspiring tale of men who read the flood and rode it to their destination? Or can it be both?'

That question I put to myself and others in the Foreword. A schoolmaster to the end, I should dearly like to furnish my readers with paper and invite them to write out their answers. Have I, I wonder, so written the story as to allow only one interpretation? I hope not, as in writing it, I was waiting for my own verdict to emerge.

I watched Fr. Lythgoe, a genuine Victorian entrepreneur, invest heavily in his new venture, with questionably adequate assets to back it. I noticed that he sited his theologate in a strangely remote place, yet one which within a decade had easy access to the national railway network. I saw that hardly had St. Beuno's opened when its priests were working to provide churches and schools for the growing Catholic communities of the local towns, while the scholastics were trying to equip the house for its Clwydian future by building up a tradition of competence in the Welsh languge. One warmed to Fr. Weld, who, though Rector for only two years, decided to add two lecture rooms and to extend the house to provide twenty extra rooms for students. Thanks to him the growth of the Province and the arrival of suddenly expelled scholastics from the continent would not catch St. Beuno's unprovided.

After Fr. Weld I could perceive little initiative in the development of the house. Nor do I sense it in other departments, except perhaps in the very slow and irregular progress towards the anglicisation and professional training of the lecturers. What of the training, the spiritual and intellectual preparation of future priests? Here one has to remember that the fundamental patterns were laid down elsewhere. The way of life of the Jesuit scholastic, the syllabus and methods of his studies were decreed in Rome, or in whatever city was sheltering the General from the Risorgimento. That is why Italian, Spanish and German lecturers were able to teach, or at least lecture, in Latin, English Jesuits in a seminary in Wales.

The general training was undoubtedly rigid and semi-monastic and its intellectual side rigid with anachronisms. Yet one should bear in mind that the nineteenth century was especially one of organisation, of systematisation and standardisation in industry, in commerce and in the ever proliferating local and national administration. Ignatian discipline, as interpreted by those Victorian Jesuits, with its stress on regularity, on fixed, known patterns, on dependability fitted well into the age of the steam engine. Regrettably, the matter and method of study looked back to the Reformation and beyond to the Middle Ages. However, within the syllabus it was still quite possible to give the students some knowledge and understanding of contemporary religious controversy. The charge was frequently levelled at St. Beuno's lecturers that they failed signally in this respect. That the charge was made at all is evidence that there existed both in St. Beuno's and elsewhere in the Province an awareness of intellectual challenge and scholarly progress and of the unwisdom of ignoring it. Similarly, the voices raised in the Province in favour of resiting the theologate in a large city, preferably London, show that inertia did not go unchallenged.

In both fields, I fear, inertia temporarily prevailed. The Theologians remained in North Wales until 1926, and as late as 1956 the study of Theology still lagged behind contemporary developments. Of the inertia of the Tertianship between 1926 and 1958 I am reluctant to speak again. Then, shortly after 1958, Paul Kennedy, who in a number of ways could have been a kinsman of the Knight Of The Sorrowful Countenance, took up his lance and started to charge the windmills of sacrosanct 'custom' and ill-founded tradition. The outraged sails dealt him some nasty knocks, but it was the windmills which collapsed, toppled not merely by Paul's courage and logic, but by the earth tremors of Vatican II.

Allowing my imagination a little too much licence, and stretching my veracity somewhat, I could arrange the figures of St. Beuno's history into two teams, the Surfriders versus the Dykebuilders. The Surfriders would include Fr. Lythgoe, Fr. Weld, John Rickaby (the eclectic lecturer), Paul Kennedy and Gerard Hughes. The Dykebuilders, captained I think, by Henry Keane, would have less stars, but more depth of reserves. The Surfriders, in spite of their brilliance, might well lose because of their opponents' better team work. The match should be refereed by Fr. Hopkins,whom I consider a neutral non-combatant. whilst it is true that he borrowed from the literature of the past, he always refused to make any concessions to the literary taste of his own period and his works helped to shape that of the future. I fear however that he might agonise too much before granting a penalty.

The match would be hard fought for both sides would believe that their defeat would be a serious check to the coming of the Kingdom. Conviction and dedication, it seems to me, blend into a fairly constant factor in the history of St. Beuno's common to the entrenched conservatives and bold innovators alike. One sees it in Fr. Lythgoe, in the Theologians preaching in what they thought was Welsh, in the refugee professors, some of whom stayed when they might well have returned to their native countries. It was behind the efforts of some men to change the geographical or theological status quo and the determination of others to preserve it. I think that every Tertianmaster had it, even if a couple of them might have been more effective with a little less dedication and a good deal more imagination. Perhaps it was at its lowest in some of the Tertians, resigned to their last year of formation rather than persuaded of its value. The same factor was behind Paul Kennedy's achievements and has inspired the work of the last decade. The perceptive newcomer to St. Beuno's will sense it in Brother Daly as, in spite of his painfully arthritic knee, he hobbles to meet them with a warm, disarming smile, and observe it again later in the meticulous work of Brother Carney in the dining room.

And the source of that conviction, that dedication? Beyond all question, the Ignatian 'Exercises', which are not merely the inspiration, but the whole raison d'être of St. Beuno's Spiritual Exercises Centre.

The Feast of St. Ignatius of Loyola, 1989,
Maenefa,
Clwyd.

Index